FROM LUTHER TO KIERKEGAARD

FROM LUTHER
TO
KIERKEGAARD

A STUDY IN THE HISTORY OF
THEOLOGY

By

JAROSLAV PELIKAN

CONCORDIA PUBLISHING HOUSE
SAINT LOUIS, MISSOURI

Concordia Publishing House, Saint Louis 18, Missouri
Concordia Publishing House Ltd., London, W. C. 1
Copyright 1950 by Concordia Publishing House

Published as a paperback in 1963

Library of Congress Catalog Card No. 63-15352

PREFACE

Like many other theological books, this volume came into being through a series of lectures. In its original form most of this material was presented in various essays before Lutheran pastoral groups in Dubuque, Iowa, Valparaiso, Indiana, and Gettysburg, Pennsylvania. Though I have made revisions in style for the sake of the shift from the spoken to the written word, the reader will probably still hear echoes of the lecture platform and will, I trust, make allowance for them.

The purpose of this presentation is to analyze the interrelations that have existed between philosophical thought and Lutheran theology since the days of the Reformation. Obviously a work of this size could not hope to touch upon every aspect of those interrelations; I have instead concentrated upon several critical periods and personalities, hoping thereby to highlight some of the principal issues raised by the history of Lutheran theology in its relation to philosophy.

As a result, the material and conclusions presented here should be of some value to students of both philosophy and church history, though my primary concern in these pages has been neither philosophical nor historical, but theological. Philosophy is of interest to me also for its own sake, for I began this work while I was a teacher of philosophy at Valparaiso University. But it is primarily as a student of theology

— and, more recently, as a teacher of theology — that I have addressed myself to philosophical problems. This essay, then, is a historical investigation of "Prolegomena" in Lutheran theology. Through it I hope to stimulate a deeper concern for the resources which the confessional heritage of historic Lutheranism provides for theological work.

I owe my thanks to many men — historians, philosophers, theologians — whose work has helped shed light on the trends and problems dealt with in this treatise. I have tried to indicate the extent of my debt to them in the notes printed at the rear of the book. In my method I have been particularly influenced by the work of Werner Elert and of Karl Holl, the latter through Wilhelm Pauck, who was Holl's pupil and, in turn, my teacher. Above all, however, I have had occasion to draw once more upon the theological wealth, much of it still unadministered, that is latent in the thought of Martin Luther and in the Lutheran Confessions.

Special gratitude is due my parents, to whom I also dedicate this volume as an expression of my continued devotion.

The Anniversary of the Augsburg Confession
June 25, 1950

JAROSLAV PELIKAN

PREFACE TO SECOND EDITION

It is perhaps unavoidable that such a preface as this should be an embarrassingly personal document, and that its preparation should be accompanied by a considerable amount of self-consciousness — especially after one has written forewords to works by Karl Barth, Adolf Harnack, and Werner Elert.

Nevertheless the dozen or more years of theological and historical research that have intervened between the publication of this book and its appearance in paperback form demand an accounting. Basically the shock of recognition that comes with a rereading of these long-forgotten pages is due to the discovery that in some mysterious and seminal way much of one's subsequent development is present in one's first book. The references to the connection between eucharistic theology and Christology (pp. 72, 73) were an adumbration of later work on the history of these two doctrines and the relation between them; the illustration from Semler of the role that historical theology has played in the development of modern Christian thought (p. 89) has been followed by an uninterrupted preoccupation with the problems of tradition, development, and continuity; the call for more work on cosmology (p. 119) is an anticipation of a still deepening involvement in the questions of nature and grace.

Like this shock of recognition, the truism that if a mature scholar were rewriting his *Jünglingswerk* he would have to change almost every paragraph is substantiated only by personal experience. It is shocking to find generalizations here that would not be permitted to stand in any doctoral dissertation, and assumptions that have not been examined or substantiated. A line-by-line revision of this monograph would probably result in more accuracy, more ambiguity, and more footnotes. It might not result in a better book. For while the revised edition would be more careful, it would also be more cautious; even as it tried to cover its tracks more prudently, it would perhaps shy away from plunging into new and uncharted territory.

The purpose of this preface, however, is chiefly to indicate the areas of further study which, 15 years after the first draft of this volume, should be pointed up for the readers of a reprinted edition. A historical theologian can do this only on the basis of his own continuing research and writing in the history of Christian thought.

1. *Philosophy and Exegesis.* The book did not and perhaps even could not make it clear that much of the history of Christian thought is the history of Biblical exegesis. Perhaps *Luther the Expositor* (1959) ought to be read as an effort to redress the balance. In any event, further study of theological history, specifically of the church fathers, illumines the creative tension that exists in their thought between the philosophical and the exegetical methods of coming at the Christian message. The references here to Luther as "an able student and expositor of the Holy Scriptures, and especially of the Old Testament" (p. 16), or to the importance of

Bengel's *Gnomon* in the history of exegesis (p. 152) were nothing more than glimpses by someone standing at the edge of the vast area of the exegetical tradition. Specific study of various individual theologians and particular issues has shown how complex is the relation between "Biblical religion and the search for ultimate reality": a theologian may be speculating as he quotes Scripture, and he may be most faithful to the language of Zion as he speaks in the accents of the Academy.

2. *The Problem of Language.* This last observation leads to a second fundamental difference between this book as it was written in the late 1940s and the form it would take if it were to be written in the 1960s. Today no book about philosophy can expect to be taken seriously if it is as blasé as this one was about the nature of religious and theological discourse. Even the book's debt to Alfred North Whitehead (which is more extensive than the specific citations would suggest) was to the Whitehead of *Science and the Modern World* and of *Process and Reality* rather than to the thinker who collaborated with Bertrand Russell on *Principia Mathematica.* A more recent monograph, dealing with the theology of St. Athanasius and entitled *The Light of the World* (1962), shows the centrality of certain images in the thought and speech of the church and seeks to prove that the basic theological method of the orthodox tradition has been to probe its key images and to organize the results of such probing in a form that keeps the content of the faith unimpaired while it strives for orderliness and system.

3. *Reformation and Tradition.* The first chapter of this book disposes of the centuries before the Reformation in very

brief order; this is, after all, a summary of the relations between Lutheranism and philosophy. Nevertheless every new
publication about the history of Christian thought during the
later Middle Ages renders more problematical the statement
that "the young Luther was influenced by the nominalist
philosophy of the fourteenth and fifteenth centuries, and that
this influence is evident throughout his life" (p. 6). Apparently this is even more true than it seemed to be when
it was written, but for quite different reasons. What is more,
the continuity between the Reformation and the tradition of
the ancient church is also becoming more prominent. This
is both because Luther's Trinitarianism is emerging as a central
èlement in his theology and because, as *The Shape of Death*
(1961) sought to show, the existential notes audible in
Luther's commentary on Psalm 90 (cf. p. 20) are vivid and
powerful in some of the very church fathers with whom he
is often set into contrast.

But for its author, as hopefully for its readers since 1950,
this monograph has served as a catalyst, provoking deeper
study and more detailed research. The historical information
which it presents is still basic to the theological issues of the
day, as the conferences and controversies of Lutheranism and
of Protestantism during the past decade have demonstrated.
The issues with which it deals are the perennial issues of
the theology of the church as it strives to be both faithful
and relevant. And the resources to which it points are still
the hope of Christian theology — the Word of God in the
Holy Scriptures, the dogmatic tradition of the ancient church,
the witness of the Reformation, and the challenging yet liberat-
ing demand for honesty and clarity that comes from the "cul-

From Luther to Kierkegaard

tured despisers" of religion in every age. If it can render such
a service in a new edition, it may continue to be useful.

The Conversion of St. Paul
January 25, 1963
Yale University
New Haven, Connecticut

J. P.

CONTENTS

FROM LUTHER TO KIERKEGAARD

1

Luther

Lutheranism has had to face the problem of its relationship to philosophy ever since the Reformation. But if we begin our examination of the interrelations between Lutheranism and philosophy with the period of the Reformation, we must be perfectly clear about the fact that Luther was not a philosopher; nor, for that matter, did he want to be one. Luther's great accomplishment was not philosophical, nor yet theological, but evangelical.

It was Martin Luther's divinely appointed task to restore to its proper centrality the assertion that in the forgiveness of sins Jesus Christ has become the Lord and the Savior, to bear personal testimony to that lordship, and thus to reassert in all its strength the true Christian Gospel. This is not theology as that word is usually understood; for theology in the usual sense of the word does not come until after this personal relationship has been established, until the Christian man gets down to "thinking it over." [1] Much less, then, is it philosophy. For any kind of philosophy, even poor philosophy, is a task of the human reason; but the Gospel is a gift of God. As Karl Holl has pointed out,[2] the Reformer thought of himself primarily as an expositor of Holy Scriptures, and he deliberately sought to avoid being classified with those whose speculative talents aroused the admiration of his contemporaries. Hence his familiar distinction between the *theologia crucis* and the *theologia gloriae*.[3]

Nevertheless, like it or not, Luther was faced by philosophy and was forced to take account of it. For, regardless of his own theological or religious stand, one cannot escape the fact that after all these years philosophy seems to be here to stay and that the connection between Christianity and philosophy is probably here to stay, too. Etienne Gilson has taught us to speak of "Christian philosophy" as an historical *fait accompli* and has shown that without at least an historical appreciation of Christian precept and dogma no one can understand or interpret the history of European philosophy since Marcus Aurelius.[4] If, as Whitehead has observed, all of European thought is a series of footnotes to Plato,[5] then it is equally true that much of the history of European thought in the past fifteen centuries is a series of footnotes to the New Testament. Even Tertullian had to know a considerable amount of philosophy to repudiate philosophy,[6] and at least since his time there has been a relationship between Christianity and philosophy that neither the secularism of John Dewey nor the isolationism of Karl Barth has been able to eradicate. Whether that relationship has been beneficial or detrimental to either Christianity or philosophy is an important question for both to answer. But for our purposes it is more important to note that every major Christian teacher has inherited a Christianity that was tinged with philosophy and a philosophy that was colored by Christian thought.

MEDIEVAL PHILOSOPHY

And so it was with Luther. As a man of the sixteenth century, however, he inherited a tradition in which Christianity and philosophy were much more closely intertwined than they are today. This was particularly true of classical medieval theology and philosophy, as represented by Thomas Aquinas. It was characteristic of the synthesis which medieval piety and thought effected between the *agape* of the New Testament and the *eros* of ancient Greece that philosophy and theology should have interacted as much as they did.[7] As the *caritas* of St. Augustine symbolizes that synthesis of *eros* and *agape,* so the many *Summae* of the medieval thinkers bear witness to the fact that there was no eminent theologian in the Middle Ages who was not also at least something of a philosopher, and vice versa. This fact, too, Gilson has taught us to appreciate.[8] But what Gilson does not point out — and what, as a Roman Catholic, he cannot be expected to point out — is that the magnificent combination of faith and reason in the Middle Ages was effected at the expense of faith, and that the impact of the divine *agape* in the Cross of Christ was too often weakened in the *caritas* synthesis of the medieval Church.

LUTHER'S OBJECTIONS

It was primarily against this aspect of medieval theology that Luther revolted. Precisely because his was an evangelical concern, as has already been mentioned, he violently objected to the fact that philosophy had been permitted to mollify theology to the extent that it had. In this objection Aquinas was the particular target of his attacks. The extent of Luther's

acquaintance with Aquinas is a problem on which scholarship
is not yet unanimously agreed; in fact, we are not sure how
well he knew any of the writers of the thirteenth century.[9]
It does seem, however, that he did not know them as thoroughly
as he did some of the later scholastics. The schools which Luther attended, as we shall see, were mostly given over to the
via moderna in both philosophy and theology; the teachers at
such schools would not encourage their students to study the
theologians of the *via antiqua*. Additional evidence for Luther's
rather sparse acquaintance with the classical period of medieval
scholasticism is furnished by the fact that while there occur in
his writings numerous quotations from the works of men like
Aquinas, many of these are repeated several times — at least
an indication that his acquaintance with them may have been
largely secondhand.[10]

But what he did know of Aquinas, Duns Scotus, and Peter
Lombard he did not like, and that primarily for religious
reasons. Though he does accuse them of being poor philosophers as well as incompetent theologians — his expressions,
characteristically, were much stronger [11] — this was not his basic
objection. That we can gauge from the fact that Luther has
rather high praise for St. Bernard of Clairvaux, whose theology
was fully as scholastic as that of Thomas and whose commentaries on the Holy Scriptures were no more textual than those
of the Angelic Doctor. But St. Bernard taught that man is
justified before God by faith without the deeds of the Law,
and for this Luther held him in regard.[12] Thus it is clear that
it was because of what they had done to free grace, and not
principally because of what they had done with Aristotle, that
Luther repudiated the systems of the medieval thinkers.

WEARINESS WITH SCHOLASTICISM

Yet another factor involved in Luthers' attack upon medieval thought was the general weariness with scholasticism that characterized much of the fifteenth and sixteenth centuries. One has only to read the works of John Hus or of Nicholas of Cusa [13] to realize that Luther was by no means alone in his contention that scholastic theology and philosophy had lost their validity and relevance. The most virulent source of that contention, however, was within the ranks of the theologians and philosophers themselves, in the phenomenon known as nominalism. Under the auspices of the increasingly powerful national State and armed with all the dialectical subtleties developed by the golden age of scholasticism, the nominalists called classical medieval philosophy very seriously into question. This was the *via moderna* to which Luther was exposed and which he absorbed in his student days. [14]

How strongly Luther was affected by the *via moderna* we can judge from his cosmology. The doctors of the thirteenth century had developed an elaborate doctrine of the universe, based partly upon Aristotle and mostly upon the Alexandrian astronomer Ptolemy. It is this cosmology that is so beautifully dramatized in Dante Alighieri's *Divine Comedy* — a universe which, as Anatole France puts it, "was so simple that it was represented in its entirety with its true shape and motions in certain great painted clocks run by machinery." [15] In keeping with its general re-examination of the tenets of scholasticism, the nominalist school also constructed a new cosmology. One of the leading figures in this was Jodocus Trutvetter, who was Luther's teacher at Erfurt. Because of Trutvetter's influence, Luther remained opposed to medieval cosmology all his life;

and though the Reformer's conception of the solar system may not have been the modern one, it was nevertheless well developed for its day and represented the best thought of the period, the theories of the *via moderna*.[16]

LUTHER AND NOMINALISM

All of this is not to contend, as some have, that Luther was a mere disciple of one or another of the nominalist theologians. An entire literature has sprung up around Luther's phrase "my master Occam."[17] Some scholars have taken a cue from this phrase and have constructed elaborate parallels to show that Luther's Reformation was an extension of the work begun by William of Occam. After Reinhold Seeberg's detailed investigation of the question,[18] it seems far more valid to hold that in the case of Occam, as in the case of St. Bernard, Luther saw the influence of the Gospel and was happy for it. The phrase does indicate that he knew Occam and probably knew him better than he did the earlier theologians. Similarly, Melanchthon tells us that Luther had practically memorized the writings of the fifteenth-century theologian Gabriel Biel.[19] Students of the background of Luther's Bible have carefully measured his acquaintance with, and debt to, Nicholas of Lyra, another of the later medieval theologians.[20] All in all, we may safely say that the young Luther was influenced by the nominalist philosophy of the fourteenth and fifteenth centuries, and that this influence is evident throughout his life.

Both classical scholasticism and nominalism were products of the medieval Church, and as a son of that Church Luther had to face up to them, even though chiefly in a negative way. There was another genre of philosophy current in sixteenth century Europe, and we shall not understand the philosophical significance of Luther's work unless we evaluate his relationship to this movement, too. The chief philosophical figures of the period were neither the neo-scholastics, like Cardinal Cajetan, nor the nominalists, like Trutvetter, but the humanist philosophers of the Renaissance, both in Italy and in Northern Europe.

RENAISSANCE PHILOSOPHY

It is not really accurate to speak of the "philosophy of the Renaissance" as though this were a single philosophical school like Stoicism or Epicureanism, for it was not. Some of what passed for philosophy in the period of the Renaissance we would not call philosophy at all, but popular wisdom at best and crass superstition at worst.[21] The Renaissance is nevertheless an important period in the history of thought and particularly important for the problem at hand.

One wing of Renaissance philosophy was the revived Platonism of the Florentine academies, whose outstanding figures were Marsiglio Ficino and Pico della Mirandola.[22] This revival of Platonic philosophy sprang up partly as a result of the influx of Greeks into Italy in connection with the union council held at Ferrara and Florence in 1438 and 1439; prominent among these were men like Bessarion, later on a cardinal in the Roman Church, and Gemisthus, whose reverence for Plato was so profound that he assumed the name Pletho and is known to history as Gemisthus Pletho.[23] Because of the weariness with scholasticism, to which we have already alluded, the search was on for a new philosophy more fruitful than the barren dialectic of the medieval doctors. The Platonism developed by the Byzantine scholars was just such a philosophy,[24] and it quickly took root in Florentine soil. We are, unfortunately, accustomed to think and speak of this Florentine Platonism as the philosophical aspect of the general neo-paganism of the Italian Renaissance. This interpretation, which has become standard through Jakob Burkhardt's analysis of the Italian Renaissance,[25] overlooks the important fact that these very same Florentine Platonists were also avid students of the New Testament, and that what they were trying to do was not merely to revive the study of Plato, but to effect a harmonization of Christian and Platonic thought.[26] One need not agree with their aim to realize that their attempt was no less Christian than that of the medieval Christian Aristotelians, or, for that matter, of many of the early Fathers.

FLORENTINE INFLUENCE

The circle of influence of Florentine Platonism extended beyond the Italian peninsula into Northern Europe and even into England. John Colet, dean of St. Paul's in London, spent considerable time in Italy, where he absorbed the spirit and the method of the Florentine Platonists.[27] After his return home, he turned his linguistic and expository talents to the Pauline Epistles and thus became one of the early founders of the English Reformation. On the Continent, too, the study of Plato increased considerably during the fifteenth and sixteenth centuries.[28] Luther seems to have read considerable portions of Plato. Quite consistently he contrasts Plato and Aristotle, generally to the advantage of Plato.[29] He even repeats, and that several times, the old patristic theory that before writing the *Timaeus,* Plato had come into contact with at least parts of the Old Testament.[30] Luther's sympathy for Plato cannot be explained by any contention that Plato is more Christian than Aristotle, for he most certainly is not. That sympathy can be explained in terms of the Platonic revival just described. As fine literature the Platonic dialogues certainly outrank the bulk of what Aristotle composed, and as such they must have reacted favorably on the Reformer's sensitive spirit.

THE "PHILOSOPHIA CHRISTI" OF ERASMUS

Another division of Renaissance philosophy to which Luther is frequently linked is the *philosophia Christi,* cherished by Erasmus of Rotterdam. European and American scholars have advanced the theory that the work and thought of Luther was largely anticipated by Biblical humanism and the philosophical speculation that grew out of it.[31]

Erasmus' *philosophia Christi* was in reality an effort to water down the pronouncement of the New Testament to little more than a shallow moralism. Motivated by the same nostalgia for the past which we have seen in the Florentine Platonists, Erasmus and his followers tried to revive the spirit of the New Testament. But because of the excesses of scholastic philosophy and theology, Erasmus put forward what he regarded as the simple message of the New Testament, stripped of all dialectic, of all subtlety, and, unfortunately, of a good part of the Gospel itself. The real meaning of the New Testament, Erasmus professed to find in Jesus' teachings and in the Sermon on the Mount. In order to make all of this more intelligible, he systematized it and produced the *philosophia Christi.*[32] There are, to be sure, certain similarities between Erasmus' method and Luther's. Both cried *"Ad fontes"* and turned to the New Testament. Both also laid more emphasis on the life and teachings of Jesus than the high Middle Ages had done.[33] But only one

who maintains that Luther's great achievement was the rediscovery of the New Testament rather than the rediscovery of
the Christian Gospel could regard these similarities as basic to
the Reformation. Luther himself perceived the difference between his theology and Erasmus' *philosophia Christi* very clearly
when he excoriated the great humanist in his treatise on the
bondage of the will.[34]

LUTHER'S AMBIVALENCE TOWARD PHILOSOPHY

We cannot claim Luther for nominalism or for the Erasmian
philosophia Christi; still less can we see in him an apostle of
Thomistic scholasticism. Where did Luther stand, then, as a
philosopher? Keeping in mind that Luther was not a philosopher and did not want to be one, we must, it seems, come to
the conclusion that he maintained an ambivalent attitude toward
the place of philosophy in the Church and in the Church's
teaching. In general he regarded philosophy as dangerous;
and yet, when the occasion seemed to demand it, he was not
at all averse to philosophical speculation.

Already in his early writings Luther came to grips with
the problem of the relationship between philosophy and theology. One of his earliest known treatises is a discussion of
whether the passage "The Word was made flesh" can be proved
philosophically.[35] His highly significant theses of September,
1517, were directed *"contra scholasticam theologiam,"* as were
the Heidelberg theses of 1518.[36] In the earlier set of propositions we find the assertion that one cannot be a theologian unless
he leaves Aristotle behind.[37] The three essays of 1520 abound
with denunciations of scholasticism. There is an interesting
passage in the *Letter to the Christian Nobility* in which Luther

forbids the study of Aristotle's *Physica* in the schools while endorsing the reading of the *Poetica*.[38] We would search in vain for a theological explanation of this passage. Rather, Luther's opposition to the *Physica* is part of the training he received in the cosmological theories of the *via moderna,* while his approval of the *Poetica* stems from his appreciation of the classical poets.[39] He scorned the metaphysics of the Stagirite and claimed that it had wrought much havoc in the Church, as indeed it had.[40] Luther's opposition to Aristotle is evident from the fact that while Thomas had consistently referred to him as "that philosopher," Luther calls him "that damned pagan," [41] in addition to other choice expletives and epithets that form a long and impressive catalogue.[42]

THEOLOGY VERSUS PHILOSOPHY

How can we account for Luther's vehement attack upon Aristotle? Luther himself gives us a hint when he says in one place that he knows more of Aristotle than Thomas did [43] — not indeed that he could cite chapter and verse as well as Thomas, for Thomas quotes appropriate passages from Aristotle almost at will. What Luther seems to mean is that the Thomistic philosophy had completely perverted Aristotle, and that because he had broken with Thomism, he was now in a better position to understand Aristotle than Thomas had been. As we shall see, this sentiment was to be of great importance for the development of Lutheranism.[44] In this context it is important to see that what Luther most passionately feared was a repetition of the medieval error by which Aristotelian philosophy had been permitted to obscure the Gospel. Since it was Aristotelian philosophy that had done this, it was against Aristotelian philosophy that Luther directed himself. He would surely have done the same against any philosophy that intruded itself upon the Gospel of the forgiveness.

Luther saw very clearly that philosophy and theology differ as to method, content, purpose, and result. In his calling as the herald of the Gospel he was willing to surrender philosophy or to repudiate it if this would be beneficial to theology. For if, as Ferré puts it, the task of philosophy is the interpretation of fact while the task of theology is the interpretation of faith,[45] then for Luther faith is the most important fact. It is, in truth, a bet against the obvious facts, a wager that despite death God does not lie.[46] The work of the theologian, then, is to describe the workings of faith, and to do so in faith's own terms; for without a knowledge of justifying faith, in Dr. Pieper's words, the Bible remains "a book locked with seven seals."[47] The theologian need not — yea, he dare not — call upon philosophy to explain that which faith leaves a mystery. Nor dare he regard the Biblical revelation which faith grasps as a mere extension of what the philosophical reason has already perceived. Whenever this has happened, faith has suffered; and this Luther would not permit, even if it should cost him philosophy. Here is the reason for his view that philosophy is dangerous and has to be watched.[48]

LUTHER'S USE OF PHILOSOPHY

But we should not be giving the complete picture if we were to stress only the negative aspects of Luther's attitude toward philosophy. For anyone who has read around even a little in Luther's writings knows that philosophical terminology and philosophical categories play an important role in much of what he wrote and said. One need only look at Luther's use of logical forms to ascertain his dependence upon philosophy, and Aristotelian philosophy at that.[49] For example, an analysis of his larger *Confession on the Lord's Supper* of March, 1528, reveals the skill with which he refutes, one by one, the arguments of his opponents.[50] He observes where they have begged the question or where they have been guilty of a *non sequitur.* His table talk is full of intricate logical and dialectical discussions.[51] Some of them were, no doubt, interpolated by well-meaning editors and compilers,[52] just as Walch ascribed an entire treatise, *On the Use of Dialectics in Theology,* to Luther when it is quite obviously from another hand.[53] They do show nevertheless that the Reformer was competent in the use of Aristotelian logic and that he acknowledged it as valid.

PHILOSOPHY IN LUTHER'S DISPUTATIONS

Equally important for an appreciation of the complete picture is the place which philosophy and philosophical method take in certain of his other writings, notably in the essay on the bondage of the will and in some of his disputations. In the treatise against Erasmus he was concerned with demonstrating that he was not alone in teaching the bondage of the human will.[54] Knowing Erasmus' weakness for the classics, Luther drew upon the ancients for corroboration of his thesis, without taking account of the potentially dangerous fact that by alluding to the Greek *moira* he was leaving himself open to the charge of fatalistic determinism, which has so frequently been leveled against him.[55] But it is significant that when the opinions of ancient philosophers, dramatists, or poets seemed to coincide with his own, Luther was perfectly willing to cite such opinions as evidence.[56] The disputations which Luther prepared for the doctoral examinations of various students fre-

quently contain the views of philosophers introduced in support
of a particular theological viewpoint.[57] One must, of course,
be careful in using the disputations as an index to Luther's
thinking. Many of them were not composed by him personally,
and even those that were contain statements obviously intended
to present theses for debate rather than positive opinion.[58] They
do show, however, that when philosophy was useful in a theological discussion, Luther was not averse to using it.

Although Luther did not profess to be a philosopher, he still
could not avoid being involved in philosophical discussion.
This was due, as we have seen, to the fact that he inherited
and later opposed a theological and cultural tradition in which
philosophy had a definite role. It was also due to the very
nature of his polemical and literary activity. Even more significant for the years that were to follow was the fact that
Luther's thought world does provide certain points of contact
with the world of philosophy. He created certain patterns of
thinking that were to mature into entire philosophies centuries
later. He also left certain problems unanswered that could
be answered — or that, at any rate, were answered — only in
terms of a philosophical orientation. We cannot leave our
discussion of Luther and philosophy without considering at
least a few of these areas.

LUTHER A SYSTEMATICIAN?

One such problem was the question of a comprehensive
theological system, of a dogmatic, or systematic, theology. It
is almost trite to say that Luther was not a systematician,[59] but
it is still true. It is also true that later Lutherans were systema-
ticians. Whatever other differences there may have been between Luther and those later Lutherans, certainly one was a

philosophical difference. Just why Luther never composed a systematic theology is not easy to explain.[60] He probably lacked the calmness and poise that seem so necessary for the composition of a dogmatic compend;[61] when he tried something like that in the Smalcald Articles, he was so carried away by his subject and by anti-papal polemic that he completely lost the thread of his development.[62] Elsewhere, when he sat down to write out his faith "piece by piece,"[63] he produced an essay which is in many ways a masterpiece, but which is not a systematic theology in the usual sense of the term. The first generation of a movement only rarely composes a systematic exposition of its beliefs; that is commonly left to what Gasz fittingly terms *"das Zeitalter der Epigonen."*[64]

Later Lutheranism

When those later generations took up the task that the Reformation had left them and proceeded to systematize the Lutheran understanding of the Christian faith, they were unable to do so without the aid of a philosophy. In a fragment from a work that is lost Aristotle says: "You say one must philosophize. Then you must philosophize. You say one should not philosophize. Then, to say this, you must philosophize. In any case you must philosophize."[65] Despite any pretensions to the contrary, most systematic theologians have lived up to Aristotle's dictum. Even Karl Barth has not been successful in his effort to compose a dogmatic work in which philosophy plays no part.[66] Thus, when Luther's successors began to systematize, they also began to philosophize. By leaving the task of systematization undone, Luther opened the way for philosophy to take a larger part in the theology of the Lutheran Church.[67]

Among those who regarded themselves as Luther's heirs and who devoted themselves to philosophy was the father of existential philosophy, Sören Kierkegaard, whose thought we shall examine more closely in our fifth chapter. Whatever else it may be or may have become,[68] existentialism is that interpretation of the meaning of life which sees it as a crisis involving the total person. And therefore it seems that existentialism can rightly claim Luther as one of its ancestors, for there are several emphases in Luther's thought that show his kinship to the existentialists.[69]

THE TOTAL MAN

As existentialism is concerned with what has aptly been termed the "whole-reaction,"[70] so Luther was wont to speak of the total man.[71] Studies of Luther's concept of concupiscence, for instance, have shown that he saw lust as a corruption affecting the entire person, mind, body, and spirit.[72] This was, indeed, the burden of his treatise on the bondage of the will and one of his chief objections to Roman Catholic anthropology.[73] By placing the seat of sin in the body, specifically in sex, Neo-Platonism and every theology colored by Neo-Platonism destroys the Biblical regard for the man as such.[74] As an able student and expositor of the Holy Scriptures, and especially of the Old Testament, Luther clearly grasped the implications of Biblical terms like belly, bowels, reins, and similar expressions by which the sacred writers sought to show the divine concern for the total man.[75] One has only to read some of Luther's Easter sermons[76] or his expositions of 1 Corinthians, chapter 15, to find that the Christian doctrine of the resurrection of the body showed him that Christ died to save not merely souls, but men.[77] As pastor and as preacher, Luther is ever dealing with the total person, and this eminently Christian, but also distinctively existential, insight is basic to an understanding of Luther's theology.

Such was Luther's understanding of the "total person." Existentialism is not interested, however, in a calm and objective description of the total person: it seeks to call him to account. The only situations with which it deals are those in which the total person is involved. Knowledge and truth are to be viewed in terms of their relationship to such involvement. Thus Emil Brunner has sought to document the thesis that Christian truth is neither subjective nor objective, but always existential. That is to say, the distinction between the knowing subject and the known object, drawn from common sense and Greek philosophy,[78] becomes worse than meaningless when I make myself the subject and God the object.[79] In fact, as Gustaf Aulén points out, it would be much more accurate to speak of God as the subject than as the object of saving faith and knowledge.[80] According to Brunner's view, it is incorrect to speak of an objective Christian truth which is subjectively apprehended; for it is not the truth which is apprehended, *I*, the total *I*, am apprehended of the living God. Such speaking and thinking bears the mark of existentialism, but it is also the rediscovery of a basic emphasis in Luther's theology.[81]

THE DOCTRINE OF THE WORD

Luther's view of truth is inseparable from his doctrine of the Word of God. Without entering into the various interpretations of this doctrine that have been advanced in recent years,[82] it seems clear that his understanding of the Word which God directs to men in Christ Jesus contains just this element of involvement. Nineteenth-century liberals who sought a *"freiere Stellung"* in Luther's attitude toward the Biblical canon misinterpreted his thought precisely because they overlooked this fact.[83] The famous words in Luther's prefaces about the Christocentricity of the New Testament [84] are to be understood in the light of the fact that the God who is the Father of our Lord Jesus Christ addresses his Word to men through the Holy Scriptures, not to provide them with information about Himself or themselves, but to give Himself to them. *"Einen Gott haben"* is Luther's favorite phrase for man's religious disposition,[85] an indication of the intensely personal character of faith.

The Word by which God creates that faith is intensely personal, too. When the Enthusiasts wanted to use the Old Testament as a basis for civil law,[86] Luther vehemently declared: "It is all the Word of God, to be sure. But Word of God or not, I must know and make certain to whom that Word of God is addressed. . . . It must strike me" [87] before God's Word finds its mark. That the Bible is God's Word even before I receive it Luther stoutly maintained; I do not make it God's Word by believing it.[88] But in the relationship which God creates by His Word I am called into fellowship with Him, I am personally, yes, existentially involved.

THE LIVING WORD

In one of his sermons Luther develops this insight in a very remarkable way. Commenting on the words of St. Matthew "And when they were come to Bethphage," he says: "Bethphage means in German *Mundhaus*. For the Church is a *Mundhaus*, not a *Federhaus*. . . . It is the manner of the Gospel and the New Testament that it should be preached and proclaimed with the living voice. Christ Himself wrote nothing and did not command writing, but preaching . . . and the Gospel was

brought out of the dead Scriptures into the living voice." [89]
His favorite word for the Gospel is *"Predigt,"* [90] and he de-
lighted to speak of the *"viva vox evangelii."* [91] God had com-
mitted the preaching of the Gospel to mortal and sinful men
rather than to angels because a man speaking to a man could
better "put over" the divine message. Hence also Luther's emphasis upon the *"pro me"* of the Gospel testimony: [92] Only
when I realize that this is directed to me does the truth of the
Word accomplish what it was intended to accomplish. The
truth of the Word does not come in the imparting of insights,
but in the personal fellowship with God for which man was
originally created and to which he is now restored in Christ.
Thus, despite many serious differences, [93] Brunner's interpretation of truth as existential encounter certainly owes much to
Luther.

THE ELEMENT OF CRISIS

We have defined existentialism as that interpretation of the
meaning of life which sees it as a crisis involving the total
person, and we have seen that it can claim Luther at least partly
for its emphasis upon the total person and for its emphasis
upon the involvement of that person. The third element of
our definition of existentialism — the element of crisis — is not
lacking in Luther's understanding of existence either. How
important this element is in existential philosophy can be seen
from the apt comment of a recent critic that existentialists all
think of themselves as Hamlet, born when the times are out of
joint with the destiny of setting them right. [94]

Perhaps the most familiar and probably the most moving of
all existential interpretations of crisis is Kierkegaard's *Concept
of Dread,* but dread, or *Angst,* is present in most of his writings. [95] Kierkegaard's *Angst.* is, however, more than dread or

awe, reverence or terror. It is the fascination that draws me to
that which I know can destroy me, it is the painful but irrev-
ocable experience of the Holy.[96] Robbed of its transcendental
locus, as it is, for instance, in the atheistic existentialism of
Heidegger or Jean-Paul Sartre,[97] *Angst* becomes a fatalistic and
at times rather morbid preoccupation with what is weird and
painful and ugly. But when it is rooted in the Christian view
of God, as it was in Kierkegaard and as it is in some of our
contemporaries, it is closely related to the thought and personal
religious experience of Luther.

What were Luther's *Anfechtungen* [98] but extreme instances
of this very *Angst?* He describes them as terrifying tensions of
body and soul that no man could endure more than one tenth
of an hour without turning to ashes.[99] Probably the clearest
instance of Luther's interpretation of crisis is his view of death
as we find it in his stirring commentary on the Ninetieth Psalm.
Here he contrasts the world of nature, in which spring follows
inevitably upon winter, with the world of history, in which
no one knows when his spring will turn into winter.[100] Luther
students will always be in debt to Gustaf Aulén for his essay
on Luther's doctrine of reconciliation.[101] From that essay we
have learned how intensely personal death was for Luther, so
personal that in order to win men from its grip, Christ had to
enter into mortal combat with sin and death and the devil. The
crisis of man's death is not a mere biological fear of the termina-
tion of existence. It is the realization that death brings me face
to face with the God against whom I have sinned, who makes
demands upon me that I cannot fulfill, and yet without whom
I cannot live.[102] This is what Kierkegaard calls "existential
pathos," *Angst*;[103] and, as Elert has shown in his discussion of

dread and loneliness in Lutheran thought,[104] Luther's theology is the matrix of existential philosophy in this respect, too.

Though Luther himself never formulated his views systematically, it seems clear that there would be much sympathy between his thinking and the type of philosophy we know as existentialism.

THE PROBLEM OF NATURAL THEOLOGY

Two fields in which theology and philosophy frequently intersect are natural theology and natural law. Since they are of greater importance for later Lutheranism than for Luther himself, we shall devote more detailed attention to them in later sections of this study. But Luther was forced to deal with these problems, and our discussion of the philosophical implications of his work cannot be complete without at least a brief examination of them.

Like every teacher who has taken up the task of expounding the Epistle to the Romans, Luther was faced with the problem of natural theology when he began to lecture on the first and second chapters of that Epistle. It is significant for the theology of the young Luther that he does not take up the problem in any great detail in his commentary on Romans, and this despite the fact that it was one of the chief areas of contention between the *via antiqua* and the *via moderna*.[105] Though he does not sidestep the basic problem, as does Barth in his commentary,[106] Luther touches on it only very sketchily in what is otherwise a rather lengthy and extended analysis of the Epistle.[107] Except for instances like those which have been mentioned earlier, the earlier writings of Luther contain little systematic discussion of natural theology. This is chiefly because his thought during this period was exploratory in nature and expository in method;[108] these were the years of his commentaries on the Psalms, Romans, Hebrews, and Galatians. Nor dare we overlook the eschatological orientation of the young Luther.[109] A man who is looking for the end of all things and the life of the world to come does not usually concern himself with the details of natural theology.

NATURAL THEOLOGY IN THE OLD LUTHER

As the years passed and as the Reformation grew older, Luther became increasingly interested in the question. Especially during the last fifteen or twenty years of his life, when he gave more and more time to historical study and therefore also to the theological discussions of the Ancient Church,[110] the problem of natural theology became prominent in his thinking. Though he shunned the usual proofs for the existence of God,[111] we do have at least one passage in which he expounds what virtually amounts to an argument from the analogy of being.[112] The detailed commentary on Genesis, our chief source for the old Luther, deals with natural theology several times.[113] Luther was perfectly willing to grant that the unaided human mind can know that there is a God, *"quod est Deus."* But it cannot know what God is, *"quid est Deus."* [114] This was not a matter of sorting out the attributes of God, as later theologians did, into those that could be known by reason and those that could only be known by revelation — as though revelation merely added to the fund of attributes which reason had already discovered.[115] If, as Brunner maintains, Luther gives more room to natural theology than does Calvin,[116] this is because of Luther's experience of *Angst.* Without the aid of revelation, the mortal man can know that there is a judgment hanging over him, he can brood over death, and he can stand in awe of his fate. A natural theology thus oriented around the concept of dread is something far different from the natural theology of the scholastics. But it does allow for a knowledge of God apart from revelation.

NATURAL LAW

Closely related to the problem of natural theology is the question of natural law, especially in the field of social ethics. The question came up in connection with the Enthusiasts, who wanted to govern the civil commonwealth according to the Mosaic Law and the Sermon on the Mount.[117] Luther insisted that this is impossible, even going so far as to say that he would not accept the Mosaic Law if it did not correspond to the natural law written in his heart.[118] Even without the benefit of revelation, the Turks had an excellent government, better than any of those of Christian Europe.[119] The construction of civil law was not the proper field for the Sermon on the Mount.[120] It was reason's function to build the State and to establish it on a foundation of law. But if reason, then philosophy; and Luther was willing that rulers should order their provinces on the basis of the best rational thought, even if it be philosophical thought. We shall see that this view of Luther's was turned into something quite different by his followers, theological and political. In any case, however, it did open the door to philosophy.

Already during the Reformer's lifetime, but particularly in the generation after his death, many of these problems arose and had to be solved with the resources that were at hand. As the problems grew more complex, those who were charged with the responsibility of building the Lutheran Church had recourse to philosophical insights and judgments. The critical years of this development will concern us in our second chapter.

2

Melanchthon
and the Confessional Generation

Martin Luther was charged with the task of restating the Christian Gospel and of restoring it to its rightful place in the Church, and this task he successfully carried out. But when the Reformation had produced the Church of the Reformation, other tasks arose for which Luther was not suited and which he therefore left to other hands. Notable among those who took up these tasks were some of Luther's younger contemporaries, especially Philip Melanchthon and the leaders of the generation which carried the work of the Reformation forward to the Formula of Concord.

The place of Melanchthon in the making of the Reformation is a difficult one to evaluate.[1] Recognizing his own inability to execute certain of the duties for which Melanchthon was equipped by temperament and training, Luther was always generous in his praise and gentle in his criticism of his younger colleague. In a familiar aphorism he compared himself and Philip thus: "Res et verba, Philippus; res sine verbis, Lutherus." [2] He thereby indicated his admiration for Melanchthon's facility of expression, in particular for his ability to state abstract ideas in carefully chosen and chiseled Latin prose.[3] That ability came into evidence at Augsburg in 1530, when Melanchthon composed the charter of the Lutheran Church in the Augustana, and again the following year when he defended the Augsburg Confession in the Apology. Despite his criticism of the Confession as a *"Leisetreterin,"* [4] Luther was willing to call it his own and in later years to regard subscription to it as the mark of true evangelical faith and doctrine.[5] His highest praise he reserved for Melanchthon's *Loci Communes* of 1521 and succeeding years. He called it the best book ever written since the Holy Scriptures [6] and urged that the Holy Scriptures should be interpreted according to the *Loci*.[7] In a moment of extravagance he even suggested that the *Loci* were worthy of being admitted into the canon.[8]

MELANCHTHON THE SYSTEMATIZER

As has already been pointed out, Luther was incapable of carefully defining his faith in an orderly and systematic treatment, though he regarded this as a necessary and useful task. He was drawn to Melanchthon all the more because he did possess that gift. In his table talk as well as in his letters Luther frequently speaks of the diversity of gifts which made it possible for him to do certain things and for Melanchthon to do others.[9] He correctly perceived that as long as he was alive to provide leadership and insight, he and Philip could complement and supplement each other to their mutual benefit and to that of the Church. Occasionally perceptible in Luther's attitude, too, is a wistful nostalgia for the serene life of scholarship which he had once begun, but had been compelled to surrender for the stormy career of a Reformer,[10] while Melanchthon quietly continued as an educator and author, begging till his dying day to be delivered *"a rabie theologorum."* [11]

Later generations have not been as kind to Melanchthon as was Luther. Students of the Lutheran Confessions are familiar with the bitter Philipistic controversies that issued in the Formula of Concord.[12] As a result of these controversies, Melanchthon's name has become a symbol of all that is suspect and reprehensible in theology. When Calixtus came out in the seventeenth century with his plan of church union, he was accused of Melanchthonianism.[13] It is interesting as well as significant that those who most strenuously opposed Melanchthonian theology continued to do so in terms of Melanchthonian philosophy and Melanchthonian psychology. In our own time, Melanchthon has again been accorded severe criticism, but on different grounds. One of the major conclusions to which the researches of Karl Holl have led is the thesis that much Lutheranism after Luther is not really Lutheran, but Melanchthonian, and that later Lutheranism filled Luther's words with Melanchthon's meanings and then put Luther's words into Melanchthon's categories.[14] Regardless of the validity of this thesis in the areas of theology and ethics, it can be supported by a great deal of evidence in the field of philosophy. Contemporary research in the theology of Luther has taken it as its aim to get behind Melanchthon to the real Luther and to rediscover Luther's relevance for the present theological crisis.[15]

THE NATURE OF FAITH

To understand the differences between Luther and Melanchthon in their significance for the development of philosophy, we must begin with Melanchthon's conception of the nature of saving faith. It is just at this point that we come to what has recently been called "the Melanchthonian blight," the description of faith in mental or intellectual terms.[16] One of the most symptomatic of Melanchthon's writings in this connection is his treatise *De anima* of 1540.[17] A worth-while task of historical and theological as well as philosophical research would be a comparative study of three essays — Erasmus' *Diatribe de libero arbitrio,* Luther's *De servo arbitrio,* and Melanchthon's *De anima.*[18] Such a study would probably uncover the deft harmonization which Melanchthon managed to effect between the position of the great humanist and the stand of the great Reformer. In order to safeguard the activity of the mind, which was his life's work, Erasmus thought it necessary to posit the freedom of the human will even in religious matters and, consequently, found Luther's position distasteful and dangerous. Luther recognized Erasmus' *Diatribe* as a defense of the mind of the natural man and denounced it in one of the most profound writings to come from his pen. Melanchthon's *De anima* pays lip service to the Christian and even to the Lutheran doctrine of sin, but by the psychological pattern that it sets up, the natural mind is given an opportunity to function both within and without the context of divine grace. In what almost amounts to a Hegelian triad, Melanchthon lined himself up with Luther and yet left the door open for Erasmus' interest in the mind to assert itself.

INTELLECT AND WILL

When translated into religious terms, such an understanding of the soul and of the mind has a telling effect on the view of faith. Melanchthon seriously distrusted the human will, but by will he meant *voluntas* rather than *arbitrium;*[19] this later was for Luther the total person, the *"ganzer Kerl"* discussed in the previous chapter. Since, according to Melanchthon, the reason and the intellect were the distinguishing characteristic of man,[20] it naturally followed that divine revelation addresses itself to them primarily rather than to the total person. The task of the Christian Church and of its functionaries thus becomes one of providing men with the needed information about God and His will.[21] In such a framework the process of indoctrination is very important, and indoctrination is taken to mean the dispensing of sacred information to the mind. The will then follows the insights which the mind transmits to it.[22] Only in this way can the Christian heart and conscience find certainty.[23] When the mind is assured on the basis of all possible evidence that the Chritsian Gospel is true, that is, that it corresponds to objective and external reality, then the mind can assure the heart and the will and give it certainty. The Holy Spirit works through the mind to grant that certainty.[24] The contrast between this intellectualism and Luther's interpretation of the nature of faith is obvious; it was to have serious consequences in theology, in the practical and educational life of the Church, and, as we shall see, in the development of the relationship between Lutheranism and philosophy.

MELANCHTHON'S HUMANISM

Melanchthon's psychology and his contributions to the development of philosophy must be understood against the background of his humanistic outlook. He was the grandnephew of Johann Reuchlin, the celebrated Old Testament scholar, and was thus exposed to humanistic thinking at an early age.[25] Already in childhood he began the study of the ancient languages and was something of a prodigy, taking the degree of

Bachelor of Arts at the age of fourteen. From his humanistic teachers he learned to appreciate the stylistic accomplishments of the ancients, and he was caught up in the humanistic ardor for ancient manuscripts and classical scholarship. When he was nineteen years old, he issued some of Terence's comedies, and two years later he began to plan his *magnum opus,* a complete edition of the works of Aristotle in the original Greek.[26] Like the Florentine Platonists, Philip believed that medieval scholasticism had not only perverted the Gospel, but had also warped the thought of ancient Greece and Rome. His task was to cleanse Aristotle from the "many absurd opinions"[27] of the medieval Aristotelians and to grant this cleansed Aristotelianism its proper place in the training of the young. The opportunity to do just that moved him to accept a professorship of Greek at the University of Wittenberg in 1518, when he was barely twenty.[28]

At Wittenberg, Melanchthon came under the influence of Luther, and this was destined to change his entire life. Luther was about fifteen years his senior and a man of overpowering personality. Melanchthon was drawn to him; indeed, he confessed later that he could not help loving him.[29] Recognizing the young man's potentialities, Luther induced him to give up his dream of publishing Aristotle and to give his attention to the study and teaching of theology.[30] To signify his break with philosophy, Melanchthon put out an edition of Aristophanes' *Clouds,* one of the most superb satires on philosophy ever written,[31] and began to teach the New Testament.[32] It was out of his work with the New Testament, specifically out of his lectures on the Epistle to the Romans, that the first edition of the *Loci* came in 1521,[33] the first systematic theology of the

Lutheran Church, published when the author was twenty-four years old. The preface to this work gave Melanchthon an opportunity publicly to disavow any connection with philosophy and even to criticize those who devoted themselves to it.[34]

REPUDIATION OF PHILOSOPHY

If we inquire into the motivation behind Melanchthon's avowed repudiation of philosophy, we can find it in the type of theological activity that he took upon himself. Trained in the classical languages, with Greek as his favorite subject, he saw in New Testament study an excellent opportunity to apply the canons and methods of humanism to Christian doctrine and Christian theology. Like Erasmus, for whom he never lost his admiration even when Luther wrote *De servo arbitrio,*[35] Melanchthon became a Biblical humanist. Erasmus had used the science of textual criticism as developed by humanism to establish the New Testament text for his first edition of 1516.[36] Entrusted now with the responsibility of interpreting the Holy Scriptures, Melanchthon quite understandably applied to the New Testament the same method which had been employed by the humanists in the interpretation of ancient classical authors.[37] Luther had denounced the allegorical exegesis of medieval times as a perversion of the Bible and had sought to replace it with historical exegesis.[38] With this concern Melanchthon was heartily in accord, not only, like Luther, because that method unlocked the power of the Gospel, but simply because that was the way a text should be interpreted.[39] The study of the New Testament by such a method gave Melanchthon an opportunity to teach theology without sacrificing his humanism, and those who are looking for "Biblical humanism" in the Reformation should look to Melanchthon and not to Luther for support of their thesis.

Teaching the New Testament did not satisfy Melanchthon for long, and already in 1523 we find him complaining that he is better suited for literature than for theology.[40] His longing for classical philosophy returned, if indeed he had ever lost it;[41] the publication of his edition of Aristotle's *Nicomachean Ethics* in 1527 marks the resumption of his humanistic work, which continued until the end of his life.

THE CLASSICS

The scope of that work was extensive, covering both the Greek and the Latin classics. Among the Greeks Aristotle was the philosopher par excellence; Melanchthon equates Aristotle's philosophy and truth in more than one instance.[42] He returned to the contention of his youth that most of what was wrong with Artistotle was due to his editors and commentators, and to his desire to bring Aristotle back into the theology and education of the Church. The Latin classics, too, received his attention. Had not Luther said that he hoped God would look with favor upon Cicero even though he was a pagan? [43] The type of philosophical dilettantism represented by Cicero was admirably suited to Melanchthon's temperament and interests, all the more so because it was combined with a masterful command of Latin prose.[44] A study of these classics would, Melanchthon hoped, have two results: they were to stimulate *"linguae cultum,"* and to aid *"ad vitae rationes formandas."* [45] Thus they had both a formal and a material purpose. As a teacher of the New Testament, Melanchthon had, no doubt, come to the realization that most of the students who came through Germany's secondary schools knew very little Latin and still less Greek. As we shall see, this was to be the impulse for his educational reforms. But because of his ethical interest the classics were also to help in the construction of valid maxims for life and for citizenship.

Such a revival of the classics, with its emphasis upon the ancient philosophers, was bound to have serious repercussions upon the construction of a Lutheran philosophy. Melanchthon was instrumental in bringing on that construction in three important areas — in theology, in education, and in ethics.

Philosophy in the "Loci"

In view of his training in the classics and his work in theology it was almost inevitable that Melanchthon should have to deal with the question of the relationship between Christianity and philosophy. That question assumed even greater importance when Melanchthon took up the systematization of Lutheran theology in his *Loci communes*. He did not intend to write a new *Summa* when he began the composition of the *Loci*. Both as a Lutheran and as a humanist he abhorred the medieval scholastics for what they had done to Aristotle.[46] When it became necessary to compile a systematic presentation of Lutheran doctrine, he had to look elsewhere for the philosophical framework he needed. He found it in the old *loci,* or "commonplaces," a term which probably stems most directly from Cicero, from whom Melanchthon probably learned it.[47] The term was admirably suited for the author's purposes in the first edition of the *Loci,* inasmuch as it was based upon the Epistle to the Romans, from whose passages, or *loci,* the Lutheran description of the Gospel was principally derived.[48] Otherwise, this first edition of the *Loci* deliberately tried to avoid philosophical involvement.[49]

CHANGES IN LATER EDITIONS

But later editions of the *Loci,* beginning with 1533, were less reluctant to let the philosophers have their say.[50] The simple topical and Biblical arrangement of 1521 gives way to a complex discussion of theological problems in increasingly philosophical terms. Phrases like *causa finalis, causa proxima, causa instrumentalis* occur more and more frequently as methodological devices in the division and distribution of the doctrinal material. In response to objections or apparent contradictions, the author often has recourse to the distinction between form and matter or substance and accident without bothering to mention that these are concepts borrowed from Aristotelian philosophy.[51] Whereas the early editions of the *Loci* were content with testimony to the Gospel, later editions contain elaborate logical discussions of undistributed middles and unproved minors.[52] Without a rather detailed knowledge of at least Aristotle's *Metaphysics* and the *Organon,* reading and understanding the later editions of Melanchthon's *Loci* would be difficult indeed.

Melanchthon took up the relationship between philosophy and theology in a special treatise in 1536.[53] "Philosophy," he writes, "is necessary not only for method, but the theologian can also take over much from physics," [54] that is, from natural philosophy. Philosophy had a definite function to perform also in the content of theology. It was useful as a propadeutic device, by which men could be led to the Gospel.[55] As has been mentioned, the constitutive aspect of faith in the theology of Melanchthon is assent [56] — not the response of the total individual to the Father of our Lord Jesus Christ, but agreement with a set of revealed truths. We need dialectic, so Melanchthon

maintains, to make the mind sure.[57] In theology, too, the skillful use of dialectic and philosophy can help produce certainty.
Philosophy itself creates certainty in a threefold manner: universal experience, a knowledge of first principles, and an understanding of the proper order in syllogisms.[58] To this catalog
the Christian faith adds a fourth, the *"patefactio divina,"* which
is mediated through the Scriptures. One can be led through
the observation of the Biblical miracles to believe that other
facts in the Scriptures are true as well.[59]

PROOFS FOR THE EXISTENCE OF GOD

Another means which the Holy Spirit uses to produce certainty are proofs for the existence of God, of which Melanchthon cites several.[60] In fact, he claims to be able to prove,
without the aid of revelation, not only that God is powerful
and just, but also that he is good and kind.[61] Aristotle must,
it is true, be corrected in terms of revelation on such questions
as the eternity of the world and the presence of God in the
government of the world.[62] But a theologian cannot operate
without the aid and comfort of Aristotelian philosophy. It
would, in fact, be wrong for him to try to do so. God Himself
directs us to the study of philosophy, and we should truly be
ungrateful if we were to despise those studies which the Holy
Spirit greatly commends.[63]

In order to equip the theologian for the performance of
his duties, the schools which trained clergymen had to offer
courses in philosophy. In keeping with his general lament over
the decline of classical learning in Germany,[64] Melanchthon
was very fearful of an uneducated ministry.[65] This fear is to be
understood in terms of his understanding of the ministry. Inas-

much as the primary element in faith was assent, the primary task of the ministry was that of providing the information to which the people were to assent.[66] Such a minister had to be a highly educated and cultured man, qualified especially in the ancient languages and in philosophy. As a recent writer has summarized: "Melanchthon aimed at a ministry equipped with the full panoply of philosophical education and supremely conscious humanistically of professional excellence. Hence ministers trained in the Melanchthonian mode became a learned and proud caste, and their theology became a proving ground for dialectic competence." [67]

PHILOSOPHY IN THE CURRICULUM

An examination of the curriculum prescribed for prospective clergymen at the University of Wittenberg reveals the preponderance of philosophical studies, ranging from dialectic and rhetoric through poetics to the *Physica* of Aristotle — the same one that Luther had repudiated.[68] Also included in this course of study was astrology, to which Philip was attracted despite Luther's criticism.[69] Since Luther had left the work of arranging theological education to Melanchthon, this type of curriculum was adopted whenever the Reformation took over in a territory.[70] And as Lutheranism began to develop an official theology in the Confessions, so also it gradually adopted what amounted to an official philosophy in Melanchthonian Aristotelianism.

That philosophy did not apply only to theology. In Melanchthon's ethic, too, Aristotelian concepts predominated. We have seen that in Luther's conception of social ethics room had been left for the functioning of natural law.[71] The actual task of elaborating a Lutheran social ethic, however, was left to Melanchthon. In his educational work as well as in his literary activity Melanchthon developed patterns of social and political thinking which were to be normative for many years to come.

Students of the Reformation will recall the political and social orientation of Lutheranism after 1530. By a long and complex series of circumstances the destiny of the Lutheran Church was put more and more into the hands of the political leaders in the territories where the Reformation took over.[72] The *"landesherrliche Kirchenregiment"* may have been necessary for the preservation of the Reformation against the attacks of Pope and Emperor and for the continuation of certain work which had previously been the function of the bishops.[73] But it was an institution of grave consequences for the internal life of the Church as well as for the history of Germany. In terms of our problem, the close alliance between the Church of the Reformation and the princes meant that the political ideologies advanced by teachers and writers had to conform to the existing political situation.[74] Especially after the peasant uprisings of the twenties, leaders of Church and State were agreed that there was need for a political and social ethic which would prevent the recurrence of such revolutionary outbursts.[75]

LUTHERAN POLITICAL ETHICS

In the face of such a situation the Lutheran Church of the sixteenth century was compelled to address itself to the problem of constructing a political ethic. It was constitutionally opposed to the political and ecclesiastical ideal of the high Middle Ages symbolized by Innocent III.[76] It was in equal opposition to the theocratic dreams of some of the smaller sects of the time, which wanted to substitute the Mosaic Law for the *Sachsenspiegel.*[77] The excesses of the Peasant War made sympathy with the peasants' cause impossible. The Lutheran definition of the ideal society had to be something quite different from all of these, and the task of working out such an ideal fell to Melanchthon. Since Luther believed that the ordering of society was a function of the human reason and since, moreover, Melanchthon regarded the philosophy of Aristotle as one of the finest products of the human reason, it need not be surprising that Lutheran political philosophy took on a distinctly Aristotelian cast under Melanchthon's direction.[78]

ARISTOTLE'S "POLITICS"

This was all the more acceptable because of the principles laid down by Aristotle in his *Politics.* Moved by his opposition to Plato's *Republic* and Plato's *Laws,* Aristotle had developed precepts of political activity that were to guide his pupil and protégé Alexander the Great;[79] these he later incorporated into the *Politics.* The moderation which he prescribes for the ruler and the prudential manner of preventing revolutions which he suggests were admirably suited to the political structure of Saxony and other Lutheran principalities.[80] The fact that Aristotle repeatedly relates his political theory to his general philosophy made his *Politics* even more congenial to Melanchthon. As Otto Piper has pointed out, "Melanchthon's influence . . . accounts for the rich development of political theory in Lutheran theology."[81] The theoretcial aspects of Melanchthon's political speculation are almost directly dependent upon Aristotle's political theory, and this is true of most Lutheran political thought from Melanchthon's lectures on Aristotle's *Politics* to the counsels of Veit Ludwig von Seckendorf.[82] By thus basing

his political speculation upon Aristotle, Melanchthon helped
to strengthen the prestige of Aristotle in Lutheran circles.

That prestige received further support when Melanchthon's
Apology of the Augsburg Confession declared that "Aristotle
wrote concerning civil morals so learnedly that nothing further
concerning this need be demanded," [83] thus virtually equating
the political conduct of the Christian with that of any rational
pagan. The ethical consequences of such an equation were
grave, and the ethical indifference of much of German Lutheranism in political matters should perhaps be traced to this,
rather than to Luther's political views.[84] In any case the high
place given to Aristotle in Melanchthon's political theory can
be interpreted as an important part of his general attempt to
reinstate the philosophy of the Stagirite in the Lutheran Church.

MELANCHTHON'S PHILOSOPHICAL SIGNIFICANCE

The philosophical significance of Philip Melanchthon is the
product of his humanistic interest in the classics and their
dissemination. It is closely related to his conception of the
nature of faith, and it had a direct influence upon the construction of both the method and the content of his theology.

Anyone who is familiar with the history of Lutheran theology, however, knows that Melanchthon's work was seriously
called into question in the quarter century following Luther's
death. Viewed in their historical perspective, the controversies
in which the Lutheran Church was involved in the latter half
of the sixteenth century provided the matrix from which much
of later Lutheran theology and piety was to come.[85] The modern study of *Konfessionskunde* [86] has been instrumental in
directing the attention of scholars and theologians to the signif-

icance of these controversies for the development of Lutheranism. An examination of some of them will help to explain how Lutheranism developed as it did, also in the field of philosophy. At least two of the controversies of the sixteenth century are of far-reaching significance for the interrelations between Lutheranism and philosophy.

One of the controversies which was to affect those interrelations was the battle that centered around the person and the theology of Matthias Flacius Illyricus.[87] In an extended debate with Victorin Strigel over the powers of the human will to co-operate with the Holy Spirit in conversion, Flacius sought to defend what he regarded as Luther's teaching in the matter. He insisted that the human will had been so completely perverted by sin that it was incapable of co-operating with God in conversion, that it was, in fact, hostile to God and to His will. Strigel, on the other hand, maintained that since man was still a man also after the Fall, sin could not have changed his *substantia,* or essential nature, but was merely an *accidens.*[88] In his eagerness to defend his interpretation of Luther's teaching against the synergism of Strigel, Flacius allowed himself to be forced into the position that sin was not an *accidens,* but that it had actually become the *substantia* of man as a result of the Fall.[89]

SUBSTANCE AND ACCIDENT

As a chapter in the history of philosophical thought the Flacian controversy has a dual significance. It is important because of the use to which the terms *substantia* and *accidens* were put. Among the opponents of Flacius various meanings were attached to the terms, at least four being given for *substantia* alone.[90] In his very popular introduction to the study of dialectics Melanchthon had defined *substantia* as "a being which truly has its own existence and does not exist in another thing from which it has its existence as from a subject." [91] This definition was calculated to include both God and the created substances. For *accidens* he gives the definition: "that which does not subsist of itself, is not a part of the substance, but is in another in a changeable condition." [92] He cited another definition, but rejected it as childish: *"accidens* is that which can be present or absent without destroying the subject." [93]

It was to this latter definition that Strigel attached his argumentation.[94] Those who joined him in opposing Flacius varied from him and from each other on the question of whether thinking and willing were part of the substance of man or not.[95] But in one view they were all agreed, namely, that the substance of an object cannot be changed, only the accidents can. If this is true, and if Satan was once a good angel who fell from glory, then even today the substance of Satan cannot be anything evil, opposed to the divine will; for his substance is immutable and is therefore the same substance with which he was originally created by God.[96] All that is evil about Satan are his *accidentia,* for these were changed after he fell from glory. Such was the position taken by Tilemann Heshusius in his philosophical opposition to the position taken by Flacius. And yet it was this same Heshusius who accused Flacius of indulging in philosophical subtleties and of introducing them into a theological discussion.[97]

FLACIUS' OBJECTIONS TO PHILOSOPHY

Flacius, meanwhile, realized that if the discussion were cast in a philosophical framework, his entire point would be lost. In his disputation at Weimar he insisted against Strigel: "It is contrary to the nature of inquiring truth if we try to speak on the basis of blind philosophy. What else was it that corrupted the old theologians like Clement, Origen, Chrysostom, and afterwards the Sophists [the medieval scholastics], but that they sought to decide spiritual matters by philosophy, which does not understand the most secret and hidden mysteries of God? Let us therefore observe Luther's rule: Let the woman be silent in the Church. For how miserable it would be if we had to decide matters of the Church by the use of dialectic!"[98] But his objection came too late to stem the tide of the controversy. Schooled in all the subtleties of Aristotelian and Melanchthonian dialectic, Flacius' opponents were determined to press the argument to a decision. And, as will be pointed out later on, philosophy won the day, even though the theological excesses of both Strigel and Flacius were defeated in the Formula of Concord.

The other important aspect of the Flacian controversy for philosophy is a position to which Flacius was forced by his doctrine of man.[99] In what he believed to be a defense of Luther's doctrine of the bondage of the human will, Flacius began to examine the presuppositions of the knowledge of God as they were being developed by sixteenth-century Lutheranism. As he proceeded with that examination, he was confronted with the problem of the *Anknuepfungspunkt* which has troubled Karl Barth and Emil Brunner in our time.[100] If the nature of man is as corrupt as Luther claimed it is, and if, as St. John says, "he that loveth not knoweth not God," then what becomes of the natural knowledge of God? [101] Flacius' reasoning here is in many ways akin to the thinking which has brought Barth to his present position.[102] The force of his speculation compelled Flacius to deny that natural man is at all capable of knowing anything about the true God.[103] If this position had become

official in the Lutheran Church, much of what we have seen
in Melanchthon's philosophical orientation would have had to
go by the board. But here, too, Melanchthonian philosophy
was saved.

THE OSIANDRIAN CONTROVERSY

The Flacian controversy on the nature of man was one of
the crises which Melanchthonianism had to face in the sixteenth
century. Another crisis, and in some ways a more serious one,
came in the controversy on the justification of the sinner which
was inaugurated by Andreas Osiander.[104] Osiander feared that
the doctrine of justification which Melanchthon taught in the
Loci was not an accurate reproduction of the Pauline and Lutheran view.[105] He believed that the Christ-for-us was being
emphasized at the expense of the Christ-in-us, and that therefore
justification was not the dynamic of the Christian life, as it had
been intended to be in the divine plan.[106] Moved by this concern for the Christian life, Osiander permitted himself to be
drawn into a position in which mysticism and enthusiasm obscured the valid objection he sought to voice.[107]

MELANCHTHON'S VIEW OF JUSTIFICATION

The fact of the matter is that Melanchthon's view of justification was a caricature of that of Paul and Luther.[108] We
have already seen how Melanchthon interposed the natural law
between the Christian and the Christian life. We have also
observed the intellectual character of faith in his system. When
combined with these elements, justification could easily become
the very static thing that it was for Melanchthon. Justification
by faith meant that I acknowledge as objectively valid the
Scriptural utterances concerning the work of Christ for me.[109]
Having accepted the validity and correctness of these utter-

ances, my intellect begins to inform my will in accordance with the divine will, which divine will, in turn, I know in and through the Law, natural and revealed. The exact connection between that justification and the life which was supposed to grow out of it is somewhat vague, not only in Melanchthon's theology,[110] but also in the kind of ethical life which was cultivated by his pupils and successors.[111]

From the point of view of Christian theology, then, Melanchthon's doctrine of justification is definitely suspect. In our own time the genuinely Lutheran position in the matter has been admirably developed in Adolf Koeberle's *The Quest for Holiness*.[112] But Osiander's objection to the Melanchthonian formulation could not succeed because of the foreign and even Roman elements which he introduced into it,[113] and because there were many who had absorbed the intellectualism of Melanchthon.[114] And so this crisis of Melanchthonianism, too, passed without seriously dislodging Melanchthon's philosophical thought from its dominant place in the Lutheran Church.

THE WORK OF CHEMNITZ

Credit for rescuing Melanchthonianism from impending defeat must be given to Martin Chemnitz, whom Dr. C. F. W. Walther called "the instrument that God selected for the reconstruction of an almost ruined Lutheran Church." [115] Chemnitz was closely associated with Melanchthon while still a student at Wittenberg in 1545, when the professor recognized his student's possibilities and urged him to continue his studies.[116] The climax of Chemnitz' career came in 1576 with the composition of the Torgau Book, which he helped revise the following year, when it appeared as our present Formula of Concord.[117] The Formula achieved the cleansing of Lutheranism from the false and erroristic teachings of Philip Melanchthon, and this was the work of Chemnitz.

During the years that followed upon Luther's death, when the check of his dominating presence was removed, some of the views that had been implicit in Melanchthon's theology all along had an opportunity to emerge.[118] Two of the views which Chemnitz combated were Melanchthon's synergism and his unionism. Melanchthon's humanism had led him to ascribe to the human will a more active part in conversion than Luther had believed to be in keeping with the monergism of divine grace, as taught in the New Testament. Melanchthon taught that the co-operating human will is a third factor in conversion in addition to the Word of God and the Holy Spirit.[119] It was as a result of this position of Melanchthon's that the afore-mentioned controversy on the nature of man began, and in the course of that controversy Melanchthon's views, supported and expanded by Pfeffinger and by Strigel, blossomed into a thoroughgoing synergism.[120] The debate which ensued over Melanchthon's synergism issued in Article II of the Formula of Concord, in which Melanchthon's stand is repudiated.[121] Under the leadership of Martin Chemnitz, the Lutheran Church in the Formula rejected synergism and with it one of the basic planks in Melanchthon's theological position. Thus the traditional interpretation is correct when it sees the Formula as the defeat of Melanchthon in the Lutheran Church.

MELANCHTHON'S UNIONISM

That interpretation is similarly correct in its analysis of Melanchthon's unionism.[122] Melanchthon's somewhat squeamish nature was alarmed at the fact that Luther's Reformation had split visible Christendom, and repeatedly he compromised his position in an attempt to heal that breach. More than once in his life he was drawn near to reunion with Roman Catholicism.[123] His desire for a reunited Christendom at almost any price also lay at the basis of his watering down of the Lutheran doctrine of the real presence in an effort to conciliate Calvinism.[124] The strengthening of the Lutheran stand against Calvinism, and consequently against Melanchthon's appeasement of Calvinism, came with Articles VII and VIII of the Formula of Concord.[125] Largely through the work of Chemnitz, Lutheranism developed a formulation of the doctrine of the person of Christ that made its differences from Calvinism very clear. His extended treatise on that subject is still one of the great classics in the history of Lutheran theology.[126] Thus Melanchthon's attempted harmonization of Calvinism and Lutheranism on the doctrines of the Lord's Supper and the person of Christ came to naught through the theological scholarship of Chemnitz and the adoption of the Formula of Concord.

On the basis of these facts the Formula of Concord is generally interpreted as the defeat of Melanchthonianism and the victory of true Lutheranism through the work of Martin Chemnitz.[127] Theologically it is certainly true that Melanchthonianism was put down in the Formula of 1577. It would be inaccurate, however, to transfer this interpretation to the field of philosophy;[128] for philosophically Melanchthonianism was still in control even after the Formula of Concord had been adopted.

THE "LOCI" OF CHEMNITZ

That fact is abundantly clear from the *Loci* of Martin Chemnitz.[129] They are the product of the theological lectures which Chemnitz began in Wittenberg in 1553. In these lectures

Chemnitz, as Melanchthon's protégé, substituted for his master on the lecture platform, using the latest edition of Melanchthon's *Loci* as a text for his lectures.[130] When Chemnitz' *Loci* were published posthumously in 1591, they appeared as *Loci* "by which the *Loci communes* of Dr. Philip Melanchthon are clearly explained" [131] and in which Melanchthon's *Loci* were corrected in their content.

Significantly, however, Chemnitz' commentary on the *Loci* retained the form and the arrangement of Melanchthon's work.[132] At no time in the criticism which Chemnitz aimed at Melanchthon was the validity of the latter's philosophical framework called into question. In fact, even when Chemnitz corrected this or that theological formulation of Melanchthon, he did so in the very philosophical terms and within the very philosophical orientation which his former teacher had developed.[133] And as Melanchthon's *Loci* formed the basis for Chemnitz' *Loci,* so the *Loci* of Chemnitz helped shape the formulation and the terminology of the many *Loci* that were published in later years.[134] Thus the dominance of Aristotelian terminology in the theological classroom which Melanchthon had achieved managed to survive Chemnitz' repudiation of some of Melanchthon's theological vagaries.

PHILOSOPHY IN THE LUTHERAN CONFESSIONS

Nor was it only in the classroom and in general theological literature that Melanchthonian philosophy prevailed even after Melanchthonian theology had gone down in defeat. Even the Lutheran Confessions kept Melanchthon's philosophical framework almost intact. As was mentioned earlier, that framework played an important part in the Flacian controversy on original sin. The first article of the Formula of Concord on original sin and the second on the free will vigorously ruled out any form of synergism or other error which would deny primacy to the divine operation in conversion. Thus Melanchthonianism as advanced by Victorin Strigel was repudiated by the Lutheran Church.

But this repudiation was stated in Melanchthonian terms. The Formula did not insist that the debate about *substantia* and *accidens* is out of place in a discussion of the Biblical doctrine of man. It did not do so because the men who composed the Formula were trained in Aristotelian philosophy as developed by Melanchthon.[135] And therefore Article I of the Formula answers the question of whether original sin is an *accidens* or a *substantia* by supporting the thesis that it is an *accidens*. The article itself states: "As to the Latin words *substantia* and *accidens,* a church of plain people ought to be spared these terms in public sermons because they are unknown to ordinary men. . . . And since among others, this, too, is an indubitable, indisputable axiom in theology, that every *substantia* or self-existing essence, so far as it is a substance, is either God Himself or a work and creature of God . . . it is the indisputable truth that everything that is, is either a substance or an *accidens,* that is, either a self-existing essence or something accidental in it . . . and no truly intelligent man (*quisquam, qui est sane mentis*) has ever had any doubts concerning this. . . ."[136] Regardless of what the Formula did about Melanchthonian theology, such a passage as this demonstrates that the philosophy and dialectic of Melanchthon retained its control of Lutheran theological formulation even after 1577.

Victory of Melanchthonian Philosophy

Thus Melanchthonianism was repudiated theologically, but by the work of Chemnitz was saved philosophically. Symbolic of this combination are the *Loci communes* of Leonhard Hutter.[137] Here, too, Melanchthon's doctrinal errors are reproved and corrected,[138] but his theological method is retained and his philosophical terminology employed.[139] During the Philippistic controversies, especially during the Flacian dispute, it seemed that Lutheranism might overthrow Aristotelian philosophy. But instead, that philosophy won a sure place in the education and theology of the Lutheran Church, and Melanchthon's emphasis upon humanistic education and philosophical competence in the ministry remained for many years.

After half a century of stormy controversy, Lutheranism was able to settle down to the task of defining and refining its theological formulations. For that task it employed the philosophical orientation which Melanchthon had given it, but it developed philosophy far beyond Melanchthon's beginnings. We shall consider that development in our third chapter.

The Age of Orthodoxy

By the end of the sixteenth century the Lutheran Church had settled most of its major theological controversies and had managed to achieve harmony through the Formula of Concord. Philosophically, too, the sixteenth century had seen the adoption of an Aristotelianism that could be employed in theological education and disputation.

Much still remained to be done before Melanchthonian Aristotelianism was to become a philosophy worthy of comparison with the scholastic Aristotelianism of the Middle Ages. In the year 1600, as in 1200, theological development had come to virtual agreement on many points; like the Fourth Lateran Council of 1215, the Formula of Concord of 1577 had brought unity to the Church. At the beginning of the seventeenth century, as at the beginning of the thirteenth, many were looking for the sort of "system" which only a synthesis of philosophy and theology can bring about.[1]

In both instances, however, the chief factor promoting the development of a philosophy was the cultural situation. The year 1600 in many ways marks the culmination of the period of the Renaissance in German cultural history.[2] By that time the educational theories of humanism had taken almost complete control of the schools in the lands controlled by the Lutheran Reformation. We have seen how those educational theories as propounded by Melanchthon became a part of the preparation of the Lutheran clergy. Other educational leaders, like Sturm, aided in the implementation of humanistic education not only on the university level, but also in the secondary and elementary schools.[3] According to the humanistic ideal, the young boy was introduced to the study of Latin already in the elementary school. This was not done by the use of the medieval grammars, which Luther had ridiculed,[4] but by means of new textbooks composed by the humanists.[5] Melanchthon himself aided in this task.[6]

ARISTOTLE IN UNIVERSITY EDUCATION

Greek was added to the young scholar's accomplishments earlier than it is today, and by the time he entered the upper classes of the Gymnasium he was ready for the study of the Latin and Greek classics. Although the classical poets were included in the secondary curriculum, emphasis was laid upon the philosophers, with the writings of Cicero and Aristotle predominating.[7] Those who entered the University continued their philosophical training with additional work in Aristotle. In the University the study of philosophy was a gateway not only to the ministry, but to all the learned professions. Students of law devoted themselves to Roman jurisprudence,[8] but also to philosophical works, like Aristotle's *Politics,* which had a direct bearing upon the life of organized society.[9] Medical students, too, could find much material for their field in Aristotle's scientific writings.[10] Aristotelian philosophy is so comprehensive a system that regardless of the profession a student chose, it had a word for him. At the beginning of the seventeenth century every student at a German university had an opportunity to relate Aristotelian philosophy to his chosen field of study.

Philosophical scholarship was quick to supply the need for textbooks and research materials which that situation demanded.[11] Melanchthon and his humanistic colleagues had indeed provided the schools, which they reorganized, with texts in many fields of knowledge, including philosophy.[12] As good humanists, they intended their texts chiefly as guides to a study of the sources themselves. In the study of philosophy the compendia prepared by Melanchthon were supposed to introduce the student to the works of Aristotle and thus to engage him in philosophical speculation.[13] As is so often the case, however, teachers and students rarely went beyond these compendia, contenting themselves with the excerpts from Aristotle given there. Contrary to the intentions of the author, Melanchthon's books became ends in themselves rather than guides to the books of Aristotle.[14] And so a cry went up from students of philosophy for more adequate textbooks. In the last two decades of the sixteenth century the textbooks of Melanchthon were rapidly being replaced by new and more thorough handbooks.[15] The Renaissance of the fifteenth century is usually given credit for the revival of classical studies at the beginning of modern times. Too little attention is given to the fact that it was not until after the close of what is usually called the Renaissance that the classical writers received the fullest attention.[16] Men like Jakob

Schegk at Tuebingen [17] were instrumental in the mature development of classical scholarship at the close of the sixteenth century, scholarship which helped to make a thoroughgoing philosophical revival possible.

PHILOSOPHY A MARK OF CULTURE

As a result of the educational and intellectual trends just mentioned, a knowledge of Aristotelian philosophy soon became the indispensable mark of the truly cultured man in Germany.[18] To an extent which our own age cannot appreciate, the terms and categories of philosophy came to dominate the teaching and the writing of seventeenth-century Protestant lands in almost every field of thought. Thus, even during the Thirty Years' War, German princes used philosophical terminology in their correspondence with one another.[19] So completely did the humanistic ideal dominate German culture in the seventeenth century that it actually delayed the growth of German national literature by at least a century.[20] The learned and cultured classes did not use German as their literary medium, preferring the Latin, which humanism had taught them to appreciate. Integrated as it was into such a cultural pattern, influencing it and being influenced by it, the Lutheran Church found adequate opportunity for the development of a philosophical system.

The system which was developed did not owe its origins to the cultural situation alone. There were also certain emphases in Lutheran theology that helped make such a development possible. The ecclesiastical and theological framework of seventeenth-century Lutheranism produced the presuppositions of the philosophical position which most Lutherans adopted. Of especial importance in that framework are two factors — the press of controversy and the presence of certain principles in Lutheran theology that made it congenial to a particular philosophy.

THE PRESS OF CONTROVERSY

Among the opponents with whom seventeenth-century Lutheranism engaged in controversy, none was as formidable as Roman Catholicism. The anti-Roman polemic of the time occupied itself principally with Roman Catholic theology as this had been harmonized and restated under the auspices of the Council of Trent.[21] In this, Martin Chemnitz had set the pattern with his monumental *Examen* of the Tridentine Council, a monument of sixteenth-century theological scholarship.[22] But the theology which Trent had endorsed was the scholastic theology of the Middle Ages, and one cannot long dispute with scholastic theology without having to address himself to philosophical problems as well.

THE ORTHODOX CRITIQUE OF CATHOLICISM

Because of that intimate relationship between theology and philosophy in the scholastic systems, the criticism which Orthodoxy directed at Catholicism offers a curious combination of approval and disapproval, depending upon the problem under consideration. Theologically, of course, the Orthodox theologians quite consistently rejected Roman Catholic teachings on crucial points like the Word, the Church, the Sacraments, justification, purgatory, and the other doctrinal differences that had been prominent since the Reformation. But in the treatment which these same theologians accorded the philosophical formulations of medieval scholasticism no such con-

sistency is apparent.[23] The early Lutheran critics of Roman
Catholicism, like Chemnitz in the *Examen,* were also rather
suspicious of scholastic philosophy.[24] This suspicion was not
due directly to their hostility toward the Roman Catholic
Church, but rather to another factor mentioned in an earlier
chapter. Like most of the humanists, these early Lutherans
believed that medieval scholasticism had not only perverted
the Christian Gospel, but also that it had not done justice to
Greek philosophy. As pupils of Melanchthon, they believed it
within their power, therefore, to liberate Aristotelianism from
the medieval perversions of philosophy. Poor theology and
poor philosophy seemed to go hand in hand, and critiques like
those of Chemnitz were equally opposed to both.[25]

Later generations, however, altered this strategy considerably.
A convenient point of division is the *Confessio catholica* of
Johann Gerhard,[26] although the new strategy became especially
apparent a quarter of a century later in the writings of men
like Abraham Calov.[27] In the course of their study of scholastic
theology many Lutherans came to the startling discovery that,
philosophically speaking at least, they had much to learn from
the medieval doctors. For regardless of the validity of either
their theological or their philosophical theories, the medieval
scholastics had developed a magnificent system. It was a system
that was intellectually respectable, and that is more than could
be said for at least some of Protestant theology by the middle
of the seventeenth century.[28] With the increasing application
of Aristotelian forms to Lutheran theological matter, discerning
eyes could note a proportionately increasing similarity between
the method of Roman Catholic theology and that which was
coming into vogue among Lutherans.[29] Lutheran theology in

the seventeenth century surely deserves the name "scholastic" if by scholasticism is meant the integration of Christian theology and Aristotelian philosophy.[30] "It may be questioned," states a modern student of the period, "whether the Aristotelianism of the Lutheran orthodoxy was so very much more worthy of the name than that of the scholastic commentaries."[31]

LUTHERANISM AND SCHOLASTIC PHILOSOPHY

For just that reason, Lutheran theologians found that despite their doctrinal opposition to the schoolmen, they could not well criticize scholastic philosophy without invalidating their own philosophical position. By the middle of the seventeenth century, therefore, we find very little criticism of the scholastics for their philosophy.[32] In fact, the various syllabi intended to orient the prospective theologian, of which the century produced many,[33] commend the scholastics to the attention of the neophyte for their dialectical ability. In the settlement of philosophical points, men like Balthasar Meisner, author of a lengthy work on philosophy,[34] refer to one or another of the philosophers of the thirteenth century for corroboration. As the realization of this kinship grew in Lutheran circles, the philosophical orientation of the Middle Ages began to wield an increasing influence upon Lutheran theology, though even the most scholastic among the Lutherans remained unequivocally opposed to the doctrines and the theology of the Roman Church.[35]

A somewhat similar situation prevails with regard to Lutheran polemic against the Reformed churches.[36] Here, too, the charge was frequently leveled against the opponents that they were guilty of fallacious reasoning,[37] and not without some cause. Many Reformed expositions of the axiom "Finitum non est capax infiniti" do not remain within the bounds of sound logic or consistent metaphysics.[38] As we shall see, this sentence had far-reaching philosophical implications, while its Lutheran counterpart "Finitum capax infiniti" became one of the distinctive marks of Lutheran metaphysics. Perhaps the most telling blows in the Lutheran campaign against Calvinist theology were delivered in the writings of Abraham Calov, a master of dialectical subtlety, whose enormous literary output is replete with syllogisms and sorites extending over several pages.[39]

PHILOSOPHY IN THE REFORMED CHURCHES

At the same time, however, a great deal of very profound and very effective philosophical work was being carried on within the Reformed camp as well.[40] An examination of the doctrine of first principles in the Aristotelian scholasticism of Reformed Germany reveals that in their discussions of questions like the relation between Law and Gospel Reformed theologians of the sixteenth and seventeenth centuries were fully as well versed in Aristotelian philosophy as were their Lutheran opponents.[41] Keeping in mind the far-reaching philosophical implications of any consideration of the natural law, one has only to remember that it was the seventeenth-century Dutch theologian Hugo Grotius who first developed the significance of the natural law for international relations, and particularly for the problems of maritime law,[42] Grotius was an Arminian, to be sure, and therefore one of those condemned by the Council of Dort in 1619 as having apostatized from orthodox Calvinism.[43] Against such opponents, the orthodox defenders of the Lutheran faith in the seventeenth century could not avoid thorough involvement in philosophical thinking; for the philosophical achievements of a Grotius are an indication of the attention which Reformed theology was giving the problems of philosophy.

THE CRYPTO-KENOTIC CONTROVERSY

Within the ranks of Lutheranism itself there were also many opportunities for philosophical thinking to intrude itself upon theological controversy. This became clear in an incident of Lutheran theological history that has been neglected by historians and by most theologians, the Crypto-Kenotic controversy on the presence of Christ in the world.[44] The chief issue of the controversy was to what extent Christ during the State of Humiliation used that divine glory which belonged to His human nature as a result of the personal union, and specifically to what use He put the communicated attribute of omnipresence. One would search the New Testament in vain for the answers to the many problems considered in this controversy; even Calov, who never shrank from controversy, suspected both sides of logomachy[45] — a judgment in which Franz Pieper concurs.[46] Actually, the theologians who dealt with the question in the many books that appeared during the controversy indulged fully as much in philosophical speculation as they did in exegetical explication.[47]

In this controversy, as in other intramural controversies within Lutheranism, exegesis was left behind in favor of philosophy. By the seventeenth century the days of eminent Biblical scholarship were beginning to pass in the Lutheran Church.[48] One of the few exegetical masterworks of the period is Calov's massive *Biblia illustrata,* but even this work frequently devotes more attention to the meticulous clarification of a philosophical point than to the exposition of the sacred text itself.[49] The fact that the great seventeenth-century theologians were its dogmaticians rather than its exegetes means, as far as our problem is concerned, that in the press of controversy Lutheran theologians would have increasing recourse to the aid which philosophical speculation could give them in beating down their adversaries.[50]

PHILOSOPHICAL EMPHASES WITHIN LUTHERANISM

All these factors would be designated by an Aristotelian as formal causes for the prominence of philosophy in Lutheran theology during the seventeenth century. There were, in addition, certain emphases within the *Weltanschauung* of Lutheranism itself, material causes, that contributed to the situation.

One very important presupposition of Orthodoxy is its definition of certainty and the means it employed to achieve that certainty.[51] The problem of certainty, which has come into prominence in recent years through the rise of historical science,[52] has had a long and spotted history in the Lutheran Church.[53] We who are the products of an age in which historicism has been as prevalent as it has in philosophical and theological literature [54] may well see the quest for certainty as one of the chief keys to the understanding of any theology, ancient and modern. For this reason men like Franz Pieper [55] and Karl Heim [56] have devoted attention to a consideration of the problem.

Like Melanchthon before them, many theologians of the century of Orthodoxy were prone to interpret certainty as the intellectual assurance that what God says corresponds to what God does and what really is. For these theologians "revelation in the strict sense means a manifestation of matters which are secret and which are hidden under a sort of veil"; for " 'to reveal' is to uncover and manifest things which are secret and which are hidden under a sort of veil." [57] *Fides humana* these theologians defined as an uncertain and inconstant faith and knowledge.[58] The knowledge which is worked by the Holy Spirit produces certainty; for the Holy Spirit convinces the mind of the accuracy, reliability, and ultimately the infallibility of the Holy Scriptures and thus creates the assurance that what the Bible says truly corresponds to what is.[59] From the testimony of the Scriptures one can then reason his way through to a complete and intellectually validated system, which is satisfying to the mind and which gives the mind the certainty for which it seeks.[60]

PHILOSOPHY AND CERTAINTY

As we have seen in the thought of Melanchthon, such an interpretation of certainty and of Christian faith made it necessary for the Christian theologian or teacher to present the faith in a manner which appealed to the mind's desire for symmetry, harmony, and comprehensiveness. But if the revelation of God in Christ Jesus, which is mediated through the Scriptures, is the self-disclosure of a Person in the warmth of *agape*,[61] then such symmetry, harmony, and comprehensiveness can be achieved only with the aid of philosophical categories, which too often obscure the dynamic of the personal communion between God and man that is the theme of the very Scriptures from which philosophizing theologians profess to draw their systems. As soon as certainty is interpreted in the manner in which many representatives of seventeenth-century Orthodoxy interpreted it, the theologian must concern himself with all manner of proofs for the existence of God,[62] the trustworthiness of the Biblical narratives,[63] the plausibility of miracles,[64] and even show, as some of them did, that the Incarnation is not against reason.[65]

AUTHORITARIAN FAITH

The opening which was thus made for the entrance of philosophy into theological discussion was widened by the continuation of the Melanchthonian definition of faith in terms of intellectual assent. The most telling index to this continuation is found in the catechisms of the seventeenth century.[66] Despite their repeated insistence that saving faith involves *fiducia cordis,* as Luther had maintained,[67] these religious manuals clearly show the emphasis that was being laid upon faith as assent in the sense of accepting facts.[68] Fortunately, their opposition to the Roman Catholic *fides implicita* prevented the theologians of the seventeenth century from describing faith completely in an intellectual and authoritarian framework.[69] But in the controversy with Rathmann as to whether the Holy Spirit is operative in the Scriptures even when they are not being used,[70] increasing emphasis was laid upon the formal rather than the material authority of the Scriptures and on the intellectual principles which could be derived from the Scriptures by a mere process of grammatical exposition without regard to whether the expositor is in a state of grace or not. Such a definition of faith inevitably involved an increasing use of philosophy in theological scholarship.

But how could the human intellect, corrupted by sin, grasp the insights that it had to have for faith? Where was the point of contact? In its answer to this question Orthodoxy provided

another point of approach for philosophy when it laid down
its definition of sin.[71] The problematics of this issue, as we have
seen, forced Flacius into a denial of the natural knowledge of
God, but Orthodoxy solved the problem in another way. For
example, David Hollaz states that "Eve sinned first, being not
more simple of intellect, but more inclined with respect to will,"
and that "it is false to say that Adam was not deceived by Eve's
persuasion but blinded by her love." [72] To this view of the Fall
must be added his view of its effect, namely, that "the remnants
of the divine image are natural." [73] Now, if Eve sinned through
an error of will rather than one of intellect, and if there are
remnants of the divine image even after the Fall, these must
be in the intellectual, or rational, sphere of life. Thus even the
sinner must be a rational creature, since "only a rational creature can receive the divine Law." [74] Hollaz points out that the
divine image does not consist chiefly in dominion over the
creatures, and that it was "not to brutes, but to men who used
their sound reason that God revealed the wisdom of eternal
salvation in His Word." [75] Man's body "in itself seems a brute
thing, hardly capable of sin," while "the beasts, unreceptive to
either divine law or holiness, are *expertes* of sin." [76] The point
of contact for divine revelation is, therefore, in the reason and
the intellect, which can function better when they have been
shaped by the disciplines of philosophy.

Under such circumstances and on the basis of these presuppositions, it can be expected that philosophy and Lutheran
theology should interact upon each other to a great extent. It
remains for us to ascertain to what extent philosophy influenced
Lutheran theology and then to seek to determine certain areas
in which Lutheran theology influenced philosophy.

THEOLOGICAL METHOD

A perennial problem in theology is the question of theological method. We have seen how Melanchthon's desire to avoid the excesses of the scholastics prompted him to adopt the arrangement of Christian doctrine under *loci,* or commonplaces. The century which continued the work of the Reformation also gave more thorough consideration to methodology. In the course of that consideration two different methods were suggested and used, the synthetic and the analytic.[77] In theology, as in other fields of exposition, the synthetic method begins with causes and presuppositions, especially with God the First Cause, proceeds through the doctrine of man and the doctrine of Christ to the doctrine of the Church and the Last Things as the results of that which has previously been described.[78] The analytic method, on the other hand, begins with the results and goals of the divine plan and from these works through the causes and events which made those results possible.[79]

THE ANALYTIC METHOD

Whatever may be the relative merits of the two methods for the presentation of Christian doctrine in a systematic manner,[80] there is a significant philosophical difference between them. It is more than coincidental that the synthetic method should characterize the early stages of Lutheran dogmatics, from Melanchthon through Chemnitz and Hutter to Gerhard,[81] while the analytic method appeared only when Lutheranism was a century old and had developed not only a theology, but a philosophy capable of thinking and writing analytically. A truly analytic theology is possible only when a theologian can presuppose considerable Christian knowledge and philosophical competence on the part of his readers. The largely inductive approach of the synthetic method could be held quite strictly to an exposition of Biblical teaching, as it was in the early editions of Melanchthon's *Loci.*[82] But the dogmatic works of Baier and Hollaz [83] are evidence of the fact that the deductive approach of the analytic method required an understanding of the problem of causality for its effectiveness.[84] For a mind that is schooled in philosophy and that consequently expects a well-rounded system, the analytic method is more satisfying, since it provides much occasion for speculative consideration of the interrelations between various elements of the *corpus doctrinae.*[85] By making it possible for seventeenth-century writers to employ the analytic method in the composition of systematic theology, Aristotelian philosophy exerted considerable influence on the shaping of the Lutheran mind.

THE PROBLEM OF LOGIC

Closely associated with the problem of method is the structure of logic. The late Alfred North Whitehead frequently pointed to the fact that without a thorough investigation of the patterns of logical thought and presentation in its own and other fields no science can develop an adequate methodology.[86] Indeed, Professor Whitehead's examination of some of these interrelations is one of the chief accomplishments of a long and fruitful life.

This fact is all the more relevant to the philosophical problems of Orthodoxy because the late sixteenth and early seventeenth century saw a crisis in the devolopment of logical theory in the thought of Peter Ramus.[87] It has not been until comparatively recent times that we have begun to understand the influence of Ramism upon orthodox Calvinist theology, in both the Old and the New World.[88] While the Lutheran theologians never adopted Ramist logic to the extent that the Reformed did, its emphases did affect Lutheran theology, too.

Tired of the barrenness and sterility of the Aristotelian logic that had been developed in the Middle Ages, Ramus sought to bring about a closer relationship between logic and rhetoric, between the techniques of argumentation and systematic presentation. His chief interest in this endeavor was a practical one: he wanted to eliminate the endless debates over abstruse logical points in which scholastic philosophy indulged and to direct logical argumentation toward persuasion and action.[89] The Lutheran Aristotelians at Wittenberg, Helmstedt, and elsewhere strenuously opposed Ramus' reforms.[90] In fact, when Daniel Hofmann, a professor of theology at the University of Helmstedt, expressed his criticism of Aristotelian philosophy and of its undue influence upon theological method, urging that Lutheran theologians adopt the more simple and practical logical methods of Ramus, he was censured by his colleagues as well as by his prince and in 1598 was deposed from his theological chair for opposing Aristotelian philosophy.[91] So completely was Aristotle in control of German Lutheranism. The influence of Ramism was, however, not completely negative even in Lutheranism; for it was probably the criticism of the Ramist school that induced Lutheran theology to adopt the analytic method with its emphasis upon the divine purpose in the order of salvation.[92]

ARISTOTELIAN CAUSALITY

A prominent feature of Aristotle's metaphysical theory is its use of the principle of causality.[93] With the adoption of the analytic method in theology, this feature assumed even greater importance, since the analytic method depends for its persuasiveness and for its cohesiveness upon an accurate determination of causes. The orthodox Lutheran theology of the seventeenth century made ample use of Aristotelian causality.[94] Thus, in discussing the birth of Christ it spoke of the Virgin Mary as the *causa materialis,* of the Holy Spirit as the *causa efficiens,* of human salvation as the *causa finalis,* and of the miraculous conception of Jesus as the *causa instrumentalis.*[95] In some cases this list of causes is considerably expanded,[96] so that even the problem of election could be solved by a skillful manipulation of the various causes and types of causes involved in human salvation.[97] Since the times demanded a well-rounded and philosophically satisfying theological system, Aristotelian philosophy came to the aid of Lutheran theology by providing the tools for a comprehensive theological method.

The philosophical influence in seventeenth-century Lutheran theology was not restricted to the external problem of methodology. There were also certain subjects with which the theologians of Orthodoxy felt compelled to deal and which they solved by recourse to philosophical insights. Like the medieval scholastics before them, they found use for philosophy especially when taking up the problem of those outside the Church and of their relationship to divine truth.

Natural Theology in David Hollaz

That problem is chiefly the problem of natural theology. Although the significance of natural theology for the beginnings and the fruition of Lutheran theology has been treated in a monograph by Ernst Troeltsch,[98] a thorough treatment of its place in the entire development, and especially in the period from Gerhard to Pietism, has not yet appeared.[99] We may take

David Hollaz as a case study for the period.[100] Because original sin "formally consists in the lack of the original righteousness which should be in a man," Hollaz maintained that there are certain "insights which are today innate in the minds of men; these are remnants of the lost divine image, testifying of the pristine wisdom much as ruins testify of a splendid collapsed house." [101] These are the *articuli mixti,* "the parts of Christian doctrine about those divine matters which are partly known from the light of nature as well as being believed from the supernatural light of divine revelation." [102] All of this is true in spite of the fact that "by original sin darkness was put over the human mind so that unless it is divinely illumined, it can neither comprehend purely spiritual matters nor correctly transmit them to the will, which is in itself a blind potency." [103] Refuting the theory that there is nothing in the intellect which was not first in the senses, a basic tenet of empiricism, Hollaz maintained that "after the Fall there have remained remnants of the divine image which are not dependent upon the senses." [104]

Definition of Natural Knowledge

On the basis of these ideas Hollaz defined the natural knowledge of God as follows: "The natural knowledge of God is that by which a man partially recognizes the existence, essence, attributes, and actions of God from principles known by nature. It is divided into the innate and the acquired. The innate natural knowledge of God is the perfection with which a man is born, similar to a habitude; with its assistance the human intellect understands the truth of evident propositions about God without pondering them, having grasped their results, and grants them undoubting assent. The acquired natural knowledge of

God is that which is gained through pondering, on the basis of the testimony of others, as well as of an observation of creation." [105]

But if this is so, why are there atheists in the world? The heathen, who did not know God in Christ, were in a sense atheists — "not speculatively but practically"; for the natural knowledge of God cannot be eradicated. [106] Anyone who would deny the existence of God would do so because he does not want to believe that "there exists a God who is the omnipresent, omniscient, and most just Punisher of trespasses." [107] On the basis of several New Testament passages and of the Athanasian Creed, Hollaz concludes that "he who does not honor the Triune God is an atheist." [108] The unregenerate indeed "cannot understand from the principles of reason the way a sinner is reconciled with a God offended by sin." [109] Nevertheless, "God willed that after the Fall there should exist in the human intellect some common and practical concepts . . . so that all men might from them acknowledge, worship, and praise God for His benefactions to all creatures." [110]

In keeping with this view of natural knowledge and in common with the philosophical and theological tradition in which he stood, Hollaz felt that an infinite regression of causes was unthinkable, and that therefore creation *ex nihilo* was to be known from reason and nature. [111] Another problem which he takes up in the same connection is the eternity of the world, an eternal question to Christian Aristotelians. [112] Two pages of close reasoning bring Hollaz to the conclusion that "the created world is in time not pre-existent, but co-existent." [113] The same human reason which, unaided, could determine that there was a God who had made the world could also accept the doctrine of the resurrection. [114]

THEOLOGY OF THE UNREGENERATE?

If all of this is abundantly clear to the natural and unaided human mind through its use of reason and philosophy, then the mind must indeed be capable of considerable spiritual understanding even when it is not in the state of grace. Could anyone, then, Christian or not, determine the meaning of the Bible by a simple rational and grammatical interpretation? This was the question bothering many Lutherans around the turn of the eighteenth century.[115] Maintaining that the clarity of the Biblical revelation was a clarity of words and not of things,[116] Hollaz replied that even an unregenerate man if he is "prepared by the illuminating grace of the Holy Spirit" can gain at least an external understanding of the Holy Scriptures, though he might never be converted; for to the perspicuity of the Scriptures must be added their efficacy.[117]

What is important to note in Hollaz' entire discussion of natural theology, which is just a sample of similar discussions in almost all the prominent theologians of the age of Orthodoxy,[118] is the fact that not only the method, but the content and the significance of the natural knowledge of God are derived from Aristotelian philosophy. In addition, so generous a definition of the capabilities of the human mind and human reason meant that the philosophers had more than an instrumental function to perform in the composition of theology. Hollaz regarded philosophy as necessary for the preparation of the soul "to grasp subtler matters and to defend true doctrines against the attacks of the adversaries." [119] Since truth is one and, therefore, theological truth cannot oppose philosophical truth,[120] even the doctrine of the Trinity can be defended philosophically;[121] in fact, "without reason as the receiving subject and comprehending organ we cannot understand the mystery of the Trinity."[122]

PHILOSOPHICAL INFLUENCES IN LUTHERAN DOCTRINE

And yet one could expect philosophy to have its say in the problem of natural theology; this is as much a philosophical as it is a theological problem. Even more important than natural theology is an investigation of certain specifically Christian doctrines in which Aristotelian philosophy put its stamp upon theology. Two such doctrines are the doctrine of God and the doctrine of the Person of Christ.

Luther's doctrine of God — indeed, the entire Christian picture of God[123] — was of a Person, the Lord of heaven and earth, of transcendent holiness,[124] who, in eternal and unbounded *agape,* is an "oven of burning love."[125] In his wrath, too, Luther's God is a Person — in existential terminology, a Thou and never an It.[126] Some Lutherans of later generations, however, weakened this insight to an alarming degree. Thus, for Luther, sin was always a personal revolt against the personal God, a refusal to let God be God in the fullest and truest sense.[127] But later Lutheranism quite consistently defined sin as an infraction of divine law[128] — which it truly is, but an infraction of divine law is sin because of the God who not only stands behind that law as the Lawgiver, but who is also directly and personally interested in the life of man.[129] A direct corollary to this trend is the definition of God which became current in many handbooks of Lutheran dogmatics. Beginning with Melanchthon, Lutheran theologians defined God as an *"Ens spirituale."*[130] Though they had behind them the example of the

medieval scholastic theologians, whose definition of God as an
"Ens" had produced the *"analogia Entis"* and all the detrimental effects which that theory had upon religion, theology,
and philosophy alike,[131] they nevertheless devoted much time
and trouble to constructing an adequate definition of God,
showing His similarity to, and dissimilarity from, the other
entia of the universe.

Depersonalization of God

If we seek for the causes of this depersonalization of God in
sections of later Lutheranism, we can find them in at least two
places. For one thing, it seems to have been brought on by
the fact that many of Luther's successors neither shared nor
even understood the impact which the presence of the living
God made upon him. In Elert's words, the peace which Luther
found in the Gospel only after long and difficult trials was,
so to say, inborn in later Lutherans.[132] As Dr. Walther was wont
to point out, this brought about an obscuring of the doctrine
of justification in later Lutheranism.[133] Another factor which
aided in this process was the preoccupation of many later Lutherans with the problematics of natural theology and their
attempted harmonization of the Christian and Aristotelian
views of God.[134] For Aristotle's God is indeed an *"Ens spirituale,"* removed from the affairs of men, the Prime Mover,
the First Cause, who spends his time in serene self-contempla-
tion.[135] But, as Pascal pointed out in his famous dictum, the
god of the philosophers is something quite different from the
God of Abraham, Isaac, and Jacob, the Father of our Lord
Jesus Christ.[136] The fact that Lutheranism in the age of Orthodoxy did not always clearly perceive that difference is due in
no small measure to the influence of Aristotelian philosophy.

THE PROBLEM OF CHRISTOLOGY

A similar influence is present in many constructions of the doctrine of the Person of Christ. The exegetical and historical effort which sixteenth- and seventeenth-century Lutheranism expended on its Christology is perhaps its greatest achievement in the field of theological scholarship.[137] The sense of historical continuity with the theology of the ancient Church evidenced by the Catalogue of Testimonies appended to the Book of Concord has a bearing upon a true understanding of the Lutheran ideal of catholicity which few scholars have adequately grasped.[138] But that same ancient Christology which undergirded the Lutheran doctrine of Christ was strongly colored by the philosophical propensities of the fourth and fifth centuries.[139] As the Lutheran Church found words and phrases to express its Christology, its own philosophical orientation was bound to become apparent.

According to the testimony of the Scriptures and the consensus of the Church, Christ was true man and had a true and complete human nature. But what was human nature? Of what elements was man and therefore Christ made up? The long argument that was waged between dichotomists and trichotomists[140] or between creationists and traducianists[141] indicates that the Holy Scriptures perhaps do not even regard these as problems. But anyone trained in the psychology of Aristotle brought to the question of human nature a keen interest in the relationship of the soul to motion, to the senses, to active and passive mind, and the other issues raised in the philosopher's brief but extremely important treatise *De anima.*[142] So it was with the Lutherans of the Age of Orthodoxy. We find Matthew Hlaváč-Kephalides, a Slovak Lutheran, writing an extensive

consideration, entitled *De pluralitate animarum,* as to whether
there is only one soul in man [143] — a problem which may seem
irrelevant today, but which was very important to an Aristotelian.

When applied to the human nature of Christ, Aristotelian
psychology was instrumental in formulating the listings and
classifications of attributes in Lutheran discussions of the *com-
municatio idiomatum.*[144] It produced long and learned speculations on the inner consciousness of Jesus before, during, and
after His death.[145] It was responsible for interesting interpretations of Jesus' saying: "My soul is exceeding sorrowful even
unto death." [146] There is still need for a detailed philosophical
investigation of the three genera in the communication of
attributes and of their relationship to ancient and medieval
psychology and Christology.[147] But even before such an investigation we may safely say that the doctrines and terminology
of Aristotelian psychology helped to form the Lutheran doctrine of the Person of Christ and thus added to the influence
of Aristotle upon the theology of the Lutheran Church.

INFLUENCE OF LUTHERANISM ON PHILOSOPHY

As is usual in such relationships, however, the influence was
by no means one-sided. Lutheranism did make considerable use
of Aristotelian philosophy, to be sure. But there was also a
converse influence of Lutheranism upon philosophy.

One of the doctrines examined for the influence of philosophy
upon theology, the doctrine of the Person of Christ, also
accounts for an important insight that philosophy drew from
theology. In the course of its controversy with the Reformed
on the ubiquity of the body of Christ, Lutheranism developed

an understanding of the universe that had significant consequences for philosophy. While the Reformed theologians spoke of a spatial heaven, in which Christ waited for the end of the world,[148] Lutheranism from Luther on interpreted the right hand of God as the power of God.[149] Chemnitz' *De duabus naturis* is seconded by many later expressions, including that of Dr. Walther,[150] in its insistence that we dare not predicate of all reality the spatial extension which we perceive in our own experience.[151] The very fact that Christ is present in all creatures according to His human nature, the center of the Crypto-Kenotic controversy, gave Lutheran theology an opportunity to realize that while space and time are necessary categories of experienced reality, they are not necessarily aspects of reality in itself.[152] The presence of Christ in the world was real, of this they were sure; and yet it was not spatial.

TIME AND SPACE

The implications of this discovery for various philosophical questions are truly broad.[153] Consistently carried out, this insight would have led to the overthrow of the entire ancient and medieval concept of *substantia* that had so plagued the Church; for that concept was based upon a metaphysical understanding of reality that Lutheranism found impossible.[154] By predicating reality of that which was not spatially perceptible, Lutheranism laid the foundation for later philosophy to inquire more deeply into the presuppositions of experience and knowledge.[155] Similarly, by its realization that the right hand of God was not extension in space but extension in power, the Lutheran Church made it possible for its sons to face up to the meaning of modern physics and modern astronomy with more boldness than has characterized the adherents of the other two great families of Western Christendom.[156] That it did not have this entire effect all at once is quite understandable, but a good beginning had been made.

REALITY AND CAUSALITY

In addition to the considerations just noted in connection with the interpretation of space, Lutheranism guided philosophy toward other epistemological insights as well. One such occurs in Balthasar Meisner's *Philosophia sobria.*[157] Roman Catholics had objected to the Lutheran view of justification and of the relation that justification creates between Christ and the believer, claiming that this was an *"ens imaginarium,"* [158] just as, a century before, Lutherans had been accused of Platonism in their doctrine of the Church.[159] In response to the Roman Catholic objections on justification, Meisner stoutly insists that the relation is real, that it truly exists, even though according to medieval philosophy it is nothing more than a *"relatio mentalis."* [160] Meisner did not fully explore the implications of his doctrine for the general epistemological problem. If we may predicate reality of a relationship that is in no way a *res,* and if we can know this reality, then the ancient Aristotelian and scholastic definition of reality in terms of *quidditas* would be unnecessary,[161] and the entire relationship of object and subject in the knowing process would have to be revised.[162] It was not until a later century, with the work of David Hume and Immanuel Kant,[163] that the problem of relationship and causality really overcame the framework into which Aristotelianism had cast it.

Although Lutheran theology was thus instrumental in the development of several philosophical insights, there still remained areas of philosophical thought to which the Lutheran description of the Gospel and definition of the meaning of existence could have brought distinctive and incisive thought, but which were neglected in the period of Orthodoxy. In addition to the epistemological implications of the Lutheran view of faith which, if permitted, might have overturned the entire Aristotelian structure,[164] there is the whole field of the philosophy of history.

PHILOSOPHY OF HISTORY

Few movements in the history of Christian thought contain as much material for a fruitful philosophy of history as does Lutheranism.[165] Luther's concept of the hidden God and of historical forms as the masks of God [166] could be productive of profound philosophical judgments. The Reformer's view of his Reformation and of its relationship to the primitive Church could be of great value in a consideration of the philosophical problem of historical periodization and of the idea of progress, especially when contrasted with the naiveté of much of the Renaissance and modern thought.[167] Luther's understanding of the place of the devil in God's universe could, as we shall point out in the next chapter, give meaningful clews toward a solution of the problem of evil.[168] There is much in Luther's eschatology which could form the basis of a valuable discussion of the nature and destiny of the historical process.[169] But for some reason or another [170] the Orthodoxy of the seventeenth century did not particularly devote itself to these problems.

Instead, the Lutheran philosophy of the seventeenth century concerned itself chiefy with building supports for Lutheran theology. The story of the eighteenth century is the record of how those supports, and eventually that theology, were challenged in the age of Rationalism.

4

Rationalism

In the course of its development during the seventeenth century, Lutheran Orthodoxy had evolved a theological and philosophical system worthy of consideration in any history of Christian or of philosophical thought. It had done so with the aid of a revised Aristotelianism, to which it had added many of its own distinctive elements. It had been able to do so because its political, educational, and confessional position enabled it to claim the loyalty of all who called themselves Lutheran.

But by the time the seventeenth century was over, Orthodoxy had lost its hold on much of the Lutheran Church. Because of its almost undisputed control of the theological classroom and the theological press during the greater part of the seventeenth century, Orthodoxy had found it possible to develop techniques of theological exposition and disputation that were often more rationalistic than Christian. The task of the theologian in later Orthodoxy was one of demonstrating and proving the validity of his position by all the means of dialectical definition and distinction at his disposal. One has only to open the tomes of

Quenstedt's voluminous dogmatics to note that in almost every article objections are answered in a lengthy exposition beginning with "distinguendum est. . . ."[1] As had been the case with Roman Catholicism in the Middle Ages, Protestant scholasticism often multiplied distinctions far beyond necessity.[2] The humbler duties of preaching the Gospel and ministering to the spiritual needs of the people were often shunned in favor of the more glamorous field of theological debate.[3]

Even more alarming and more dangerous than this emphasis upon formal theology was the extent to which the use of reason began to dominate the theology of confessional Orthodoxy. We have seen how David Hollaz, a representative dogmatician, felt capable of demonstrating by the use of reason alone that there was a God, that He was good and kind to His creatures, that He had created the world *ex nihilo,* that there was a resurrection of the body; not even the mystery of the Holy Trinity could contradict philosophy. In an effort to demonstrate the plausibility of the Christian faith, many Orthodox theologians made extravagant claims for reason and philosophy, so that to many an observer it must have seemed that there was very little actually remaining for divine revelation to supply after philosophy had done its best to discover the true nature of reality. How dangerous this was for the future of Lutheranism we shall see a little later on.

LUTHERANISM AND THE COMMON PEOPLE

Any theology which permits itself to be drawn into such a position cannot long hold the loyalty of a church. The people had grown weary of the endless and useless theological disputes in which their pastors and professors engaged.[4] But,

apparently unmindful of the threatening doom, Lutheran Orthodoxy became more and more abstract as the year 1700
arrived and passed. Meanwhile, true and vital Christianity was
too often neglected. One of the safeguards which Orthodox
theologians like Johann Gerhard had set up against a destructive intellectualism was their doctrine of the internal testimony
of the Holy Spirit.[5] Although they opposed the Quakers and
other advocates of the inner light for their emotionalism and
subjectivism,[6] they still sensed the need for the personal assurance of salvation which is so obviously promised in the New
Testament. As modern articulations of the doctrine have shown,
the Orthodox view of the testimony of the Holy Spirit can be
a powerful religious dynamic.[7] But toward the close of the
seventeenth century this curb against intellectualism was receiving less and less attention in the dogmatic manuals of the
Lutheran Church.[8]

The Neglect of Missions

At the same time the Lutheran Church neglected the missionary enterprise. Professor Latourette has listed several reasons for this lack of interest in missions — anti-Roman polemics, eschatology, religious wars, the State churches, absence of
monks in Protestantism, lack of contact with non-Christian
peoples.[9] Werner Elert has ascribed it to the fact that according to the imperfect geographical knowledge of the Reformation most Protestants were under the impression that the Gospel had already been brought to all the inhabitable portions of
the earth's surface.[10] Whatever may have been the reasons
behind the situation, it is certainly indicative of church conditions in seventeenth-century Germany that the leaders of Lutheranism found time, opportunity, and funds for extensive

theological debate and publication,[11] but none for missions. Some of them, in fact, maintained that the Great Commission was intended only for the Apostles.[12]

Closely parallel to these developments is the decline in the ethical consciousness of the Lutheran Church.[13] A detailed examination of the ethics of Johann Gerhard indicates how the impulses received from the Reformation were codified in the theological work of the Orthodox period.[14] It also shows that many of these impulses were being weakened,[15] and after Gerhard the weakening process was speeded up. With the disappearance of the *locus "De charitate"* in dogmatics[16] and with the separation of dogmatics and ethics,[17] the theological scholarship of the Church contented itself increasingly with doctrinal articulation and the defense of the Lutheran position. This neglect of ethics in theory was too often matched by a similar neglect in practice.[18]

THE THIRTY YEARS' WAR

While all of this was going on, the people of Germany were passing through the crisis of the Thirty Years' War and the postwar period. Curiously, few histories of Lutheran theology do more than mention the Thirty Years' War,[19] which thoroughly decimated the population of Germany and set her back at least a century. That is indicative of the fact that a large section of Lutheran theology scarcely took notice of the fiery trial through which the people were passing,[20] another index of how completely much of Orthodox theology had lost touch with the people, even though the Church's hymnody did keep pace with the people's need.[21]

As Lutheran Orthodoxy was losing its hold on the people during the late seventeenth and early eighteenth century, other movements began to claim their loyalty. Religiously, the decline in the prestige of Orthodoxy accounts for the increasing number of sects, many of them eschatologically oriented, that sprang up during the war and the period of reconstruction.[22] Philosophically, many of those who could not find satisfaction in the Orthodox synthesis turned to the theosophy of men like Boehme [23] or the spiritualism of Gottfried Arnold.[24] Erich Seeberg's detailed analysis of Gottfried Arnold's thought has given us an understanding of how the systematizers of Orthodoxy could no longer control the thinking of seventeenth-century Germany and of why the philosophies of men like Arnold grew in popularity.[25]

The Rise of Pietism

There was another movement in the late seventeenth century which found no satisfaction in Orthodoxy and which tried to develop a substitute. That movement was Pietism.[26] The causes of the Pietist movement lie deep within the political and parochial life of Germany,[27] but from what has already been said it seems clear that Pietism represented a legitimate protest against the excesses of the Orthodox period. The moral level of the German people was certainly at a low ebb.[28] Christian faith had been equated with intellectual assent to a body of revealed truth for so long that the Christian way of life received far less than its share of attention. If the sermons of the seventeenth century that have appeared in print are any sample,[29] the type of preaching to which the people were being exposed was unproductive of religious, spiritual, or ethical power. It was against this situation that Spener leveled his protest.[30] He sought a reorientation of the Christian faith in terms of personal relationship, a return to many of the Reformation's religious insights that had gradually been obscured,[31] and a restatement of the vitality of the Christian Gospel in its dynamic relevance for the everyday problems of the everyday man.

Recent studies have shown the wide circle of influence over which Pietism was felt.[32] The missionary achievements of the movement are well known.[33] Less familiar are the contributions which Pietism made to the beginnings of German national literature in opposition to the stilted Latinity cultivated by many of the leaders of Orthodoxy.[34] Important in that connection is the hymnological activity of many Pietistic Lutherans.[35] On the basis of research that has been carried on we are now in a position to evaluate the connection between Pietism and the nascent German nationalism of the late seventeenth and especially of the eighteenth century.[36] And so Pietism was by no means the sterile movement it is sometimes painted to be.

PIETISM AND THEOLOGY

The fact remains, however, that by the very nature of its opposition to Orthodoxy, Pietism was unable to effect either a theological or a philosophical reconstruction, thus leaving the field open to the Rationalism that was to follow. The founders of Pietism, Spener and Francke, were men of no mean scholarly ability.[37] Their successors were much more interested in repairing the damages of the past one hundred years than in theological, let alone philosophical, scholarship.[38] Besides, the political situation, as well as the danger of being identified with the sectarians, made it mandatory for the Pietists to insist that, doctrinally at least, they were still loyal adherents of orthodox

Lutheranism. J. G. Walch's extensive history of the theological controversies within the Lutheran Church, composed during the storm and stress of the Pietistic period, bears witness to the fact that many of the Pietists did not succeed in this insistence.[39] Thus one antagonist accused the Pietists of reviving the Osiandrian heresy.[40] Precisely because they were on the defensive theologically, the Pietists never got around to the composition of a theological system. Except for isolated masterpieces like Bengel's commentary on the New Testament,[41] men of Pietistic inclination left scientific theological work to the Orthodox. It is perhaps symptomatic of the situation that Spener is almost exactly contemporary with Hollaz.[42]

Because of this situation and because Rationalism followed soon afterwards, it has become customary to maintain that Pietism so debilitated Lutheranism that Rationalism had little difficulty in taking over.[43] Such an interpretation neglects the very important fact that, philosophically speaking, there is much affinity between the rationalism of Lutheran Orthodoxy and the epistemological principles of the Age of Reason, and that at least part of the historical continuity of Rationalism is to be found in this affinity.[44] A much more accurate estimate than the usual one seems to be the judgment of one of our contemporaries that "even as Pietistic Subjectivism in certain extreme characteristics leads through the very heart of the 'inner light' to the rationalistic principle, so the extreme Intellectualism of late Orthodoxy prepared the way for the Age of Reason."[45] Since Pietism was incapable of developing a new theology more suited to the needs of the time, Orthodoxy held control of the theological schools until Rationalism was sufficiently developed to take over.

From Orthodoxy to Rationalism

The transition from late Orthodoxy to early Rationalism is barely perceptible, inasmuch as Orthodoxy was rationalistic and Rationalism tried to remain orthodox.[46] Early eighteenth-century Rationalism tried to retain the authority of the Biblical revelation and to do so in Orthodoxy's terms. As we have pointed out, Orthodoxy had regarded many distinctively Christian tenets as capable of rational demonstration and had offered such demonstration. According to Orthodoxy it was more rational to accept the Biblical record as trustworthy than to reject it. No thinking man could honestly deny the Bible's claims to authority. No philosopher who was true to philosophy and to the sound workings of the human reason could seriously question the basic presuppositions and claims of the Christian faith.[47]

Many leaders of early eighteenth-century thought took Orthodoxy at its word on this point and set out to prove the validity and accuracy of the Bible. We have seen that Melanchthon applied the canons of humanistic interpretation to the Biblical text,[48] and that the age of Orthodoxy claimed such clarity for the Bible that even an unregenerate person, with sufficient philological ability, could find the true meaning of the Scriptures.[49] From this claim it was an easy step to the position taken by Johann August Ernesti of Leipzig, whose handbook on the interpretation of the New Testament is a landmark in the history of hermeneutics.[50] In this work Ernesti maintained that the Bible is to be interpreted in the same manner as other works of antiquity: it is to be judged textually, historically, and philologically, and thus the interpreter derives the correct meaning from the text.

JOHANN DAVID MICHAELIS

Ernesti's contemporary Johann David Michaelis devoted most
of his long career to an attempt to demonstrate the trustworthiness of the Bible.[51] With truly stupendous scholarly attain-
ments at his command, Michaelis tried to prove from miracles,
from prophecies, from historical records, and from nature that
the Bible must be worthy of credence.[52] Both he and Ernesti
clung to the doctrine of the verbal inspiration of the Scriptures
and to the reality of the supernatural element in faith and life.[53]
But they had learned from Orthodoxy that the Bible did not
depend for authentication merely upon God and His witness to
Himself in the Holy Spirit. The external proofs for the superiority of Christianity were supposed to be strong enough to convince any open-minded and rational person, and it was to these
external proofs that the early Rationalists devoted themselves.[54]

While the early proponents of Rationalism were thus at-
tempting to use reason in defense of revelation, a new Christian
philosophy was being developed by Gottfried Wilhelm von
Leibniz and his followers.[55] The currently popular organic
philosophy of Whitehead has served to call attention to some
of the neglected aspects of Leibniz, who anticipated certain
insights of Whitehead's metaphysics.[56] The new attention being
given to Leibniz in our time has already produced several significant studies, with many more to come.[57] One of the problems
that will have to be treated before we can adequately evaluate
Leibniz' place in the history of thought is his debt to Christian,
specifically Lutheran, theology.[58] Because of the theory, now
quite thoroughly discredited, that Leibniz joined the Roman
Catholic Church before his death,[59] many students of the history
of philosophy have overlooked his Lutheran background and
training.

LEIBNIZ AND LUTHERANISM

In the absence of a detailed analysis of Leibniz' relation to Lutheran theology [60] we may nevertheless suppose that his affinity for scholasticism was derived, not primarily from the medieval scholastics,[61] but from the Protestant scholastics who were his early teachers. Scherzer and Jakob Thomasius influenced the young Leibniz, as did the great Lutheran theologian Abraham Calov.[62] Leibniz' first literary attempt was a dissertation on the problem of individuation,[63] to which he addressed himself again later on in his *Monadologie* of 1714.[64] But individuation was a question to which Protestant scholasticism, both Lutheran and Reformed, had devoted a great deal of attention,[65] even inquiring, as we have seen, into the problem of the plurality of souls.[66] What has been termed Leibniz' "spiritual pluralism" [67] may well have its roots in the interpretation which men like Balthasar Meisner gave to the ancient theories of substance and of matter.[68] His writings use terms like *causa deficiens, potentia obedientalis,* and similar phrases derived from the Aristotelian scholasticism of Lutheran Orthodoxy,[69] and his distinction between conditioned and unconditioned necessity [70] seems to come from the same source.[71]

Much clearer than the dependence of Leibniz' monadological speculations upon Lutheran sources [72] is the influence of Lutheranism upon his best-known work, the *Théodicée* of 1710. The purpose of this book, as announced in the title, was to discover the relation between the goodness of God, the free will of man, and the presence of evil in the world.[73] In his introduction to the *Théodicée* Leibniz takes up the problem of faith and reason.[74] He is intensely critical of those who, like Descartes, had made a cleavage between faith and philosophy.[75]

Over against the distinction between philosophical and religious truth, Leibniz insisted upon the conformity of the truths of faith and those of philosophy.[76] When he tried to justify the ways of God to man in the *Théodicée,* he combined the teachings and techniques of theology and philosophy to prove that God's will is done.[77] Like the theologians of Orthodoxy, Leibniz grounded his defense of the goodness of God in the assertion that God could not act in a manner contrary to His being and will.[78] What modern historians of philosophy have found objectionable in the philosophy of Leibniz is not so much his opposition to empiricism [79] as his strenuous effort to be both a Christian and a philosopher in his solution of the problem of evil.[80]

THE WORK OF WOLFF

It was Leibniz' ambition to construct a harmonization of reason and revelation which would do justice to both the teachings of the Christian faith and the valid judgments of philosophy.[81] The introductory essay of the *Théodicée* had been a step in the direction of such a harmonization. But Leibniz did not have an opportunity to think through the ramifications of his views on the relation of faith and reason and thus was unable to fulfill his ambition of a mathematically precise delineation of this question. The inadequate answer which he left [82] was developed by his followers, especially by Christian von Wolff.[83] Like many pupils, however, Wolff neither removed the inconsistencies in his master's system nor even did justice to the more profound insights which Leibniz had developed.[84]

Taking up Leibniz' suggestion that the harmony of reason and revelation could be demonstrated mathematically, Wolff evolved a system that was neither good philosophy nor good theology.[85] "I have always wished," he writes, "that theology and philosophy should not be confused with each other, and I am convinced that if one finds the truth in each, they cannot oppose each other. For if theology said no more than what the Scriptures teach and did not wish to add what they do not teach, and if philosophy remained with that which can be demonstrated from reason, then the difference between supernatural and natural truth would become clearer, the superiority of revealed religion over natural would become more evident, and many a controversy would be avoided which has arisen through the untimely mingling of philosophy and theology." [86] But in practice he did not carry out this assertion,[87] and both his philosophy and his theology became a barren rationalism, excluding the distinctive elements of Christianity as well as many of the valuable doctrines of Leibniz' philosophy.[88]

RATIONALISM IN ENGLAND AND FRANCE

Wolff's difficulties in retaining Christianity within a rationalistic framework presaged the situation in which all of Rationalism soon found itself. For while the early German rationalists had been striving to harmonize the Christian faith and rationalistic philosophy, their contemporaries in England and France had long since surrendered that attempt and had developed a *rationalismus vulgaris,* which frankly broke with Christian revelation.[89] Herbert of Cherbury had enunciated the five points which were to be the charter of English Deism and had demanded the reduction of all religion to the minimal assertions of this charter.[90] By the eighteenth century, Deism had taken control of the minds of many English intellectuals and had cut deeply into the life of the Church of England.[91] In France a similar movement was under way. The Encyclopedic movement, which helped lay the foundation for the destruction of the ancient regime, the nature philosophy of Rousseau, the wit of Voltaire — all these are aspects of the general revolt of eighteenth-century French culture against the Christian faith and of the substitution of the "heavenly city of the philosophers" in this life for the promise of the heavenly City of God that was to come.[92]

Both English Deism and the French *philosophes* found sympathy and support in Germany.[93] When Frederick the Great assumed the Prussian throne in 1740, their influence and prestige were greatly enhanced. Frederick was in close personal contact with Voltaire and other leaders of the French movement,[94] and though the child of a Christian home, the monarch held to a philosophy best described as Deism.[95] In spite of his studied tolerance of all religious beliefs and sects and his attempt to treat all of them fairly,[96] Frederick's philosophy helped to prepare the way for a thoroughgoing rationalism to take control of the German educated classes as well as of much of the German Church.

THE THEOLOGY OF SEMLER

A pathetic example of the plight in which eighteenth-century Rationalism found itself is Johann Salomon Semler.[97] Semler was deeply interested in retaining the authority of the Bible and the religiousness that grew out of Biblical faith.[98] In his personal devotional life and in the family circle he cultivated a deep and Christian piety.[99] But in his theology he

adopted and used rationalistic principles. Orthodoxy had maintained that the Bible could be buttressed by honest historical
investigation of the formation and make-up of the Biblical
canon.[100] When Semler attempted just such an investigation,
he came to radically different conclusions from those of Orthodoxy. His study of the history of the Old and the New
Testament canons brought him to the view that the origins of
the Scriptures were not, as Orthodoxy maintained, completely
divine, but that the human factor had entered into the selection
of the Biblical books.[101]

In its defense of the Bible, Orthodoxy had also maintained
that a reading of the contents of the Scriptures was sufficient to
convince any rational person of the accuracy of the Scriptural
narrative.[102] Semler found that such reading produced exactly
the opposite effect in him. In his desperation he worked out
an accommodationistic theory of inspiration, contending that the
Holy Spirit adapted Himself to the geographical, scientific, and
historical mistakes of the Biblical writers.[103] Orthodoxy had
linked its theology with an intellectualistic philosophy and had
claimed support from that philosophy for its theological insights. When men like Semler were no longer able to give
support to the philosophy, the theology, too, was discarded.
Semler did not want to substitute philosophy for theology.[104]
Repeatedly in his writings he pleads for the autonomy of
theology and insists that theology must be Biblical rather than
philosophical.[105] But he was so thoroughly under the influence
of the Rationalism from which he came that his philosophical
analyses continually challenged the religious and theological
opinions he cherished and wished to keep.[106]

LESSING'S PHILOSOPHY

Only one more step was needed from Semler to a complete Rationalism. That step came in the movement usually linked with the name of the German dramatist Gotthold Ephraim Lessing.[107] Coming from an old Lutheran family, Lessing was well versed in Lutheran doctrine.[108] His father composed a defense of Luther on the occasion of the bicentennial of the Reformation in 1717. Its thoughts reflect a broad, but still positive, Christianity.[109] The more famous son departed from the faith of his father. As his *Nathan der Weise* shows, Gotthold Ephraim Lessing denied any abiding distinctiveness to Christianity.[110] In its stead he proposed a Deistic philosophy of morality and of faith in a Supreme Being. Nothing was to be believed which could not be rationally validated.[111] Lessing's philosophy gained adherence among the people through its association with the popular literature of the time and its incorporation in the voluminous *Allgemeine deutsche Bibliothek,* published in the latter part of the eighteenth century.[112] His movement was as opposed to the rationalistic theology of the time as to the older Orthodoxy; Lessing referred to the rationalistic theologians contemptuously as *"Halbphilosophen."* [113]

THE DOMINANCE OF RATIONALISM

Thus the proud Rationalism of the Enlightenment assumed a dominant position in the life of Lutheran lands. Supremely confident of reason's ability to discover the ultimate nature of reality and to work out an adequate philosophy of life, the rationalistic philosophers refused the aid of a theology which could at best only substantiate that which reason had long since grasped and, at worst, could becloud it with all manner of superstition and ignorance. Some of the Rationalists found that reason left to itself even in matters of morality frequently ended in a weak relativism that threatened the bases of social living. The potential ethical crisis which Rationalism thus precipitated was temporarily checked by the fortunate inconsistency which prevented most Rationalists from carrying out the ethical implications of their metaphysical judgments.

Such was the situation when Immanuel Kant of Koenigsberg appeared on the scene. He was the product of a Pietistic home;[114] and despite his later revulsion from many of the excesses of Pietism,[115] he retained a respect for the resoluteness and trust in Providence which that movement bred in its adherents.[116] In the *Collegium Fridericianum* of Koenigsberg he was trained in Lutheran doctrine. His pastor, F. A. Schultz, seems to have recognized the boy's intellectual ability and to have encouraged him in his studies. As rector of the college, he exerted a strong influence on the young Kant during the eight years which the boy spent there.[117] Schultz was a Pietist in his practical religious teaching and ministry, but remained Orthodox in his theology.[118] At his urging, and perhaps in fulfillment of a deathbed wish of his mother,[119] Kant entered the University of Koenigsberg, apparently matriculating in theology. After some time he discontinued his theological studies and devoted his chief attention to philosophy, with special emphasis upon the metaphysical implications of the natural sciences.[120] Here he received inspiration from a young member of the University faculty, Martin Knutzen, who was seeking to correct the errors of Christian Wolff by drawing upon Newtonian physics.[121] Kant never completely escaped these influences of his youth, and many of his writings bear the unmistakable traces of his Pietistic and Lutheran upbringing.[122]

LUTHERAN INFLUENCES IN KANT

Those traces are evident also in some of Kant's outstanding philosophical achievements. There are, for example, some remarkable affinities between Kant's *Critique of Pure Reason* and Lutheran theology. At its best, Lutheran theology has always maintained that the true meaning of existence lies beyond the reach of human reason, that the life of the believer is "hid with Christ in God." [123] Kant's refutation of rationalistic epistemology in the *Critique* is as destructive of the Orthodox theory of knowledge as it is of the Rationalism of the eighteenth century.[124] But for just that reason it serves to emphasize an insight of Luther's that Orthodoxy had all but forgotten: that faith is not a considered step based upon the best available evidence, but a leap into the arms of God. The artificial system of proofs and guarantees that Melanchthon and his followers had set up to buttress Christianity was based upon a false understanding of the relationship between reason and reality, false philosophically as well as theologically. One by one, Kant's *Critique* does away with the elaborate proofs for the existence of God which Lutheran Aristotelianism shared with medieval scholasticism.[125] For this fact, scholasticism has never forgiven Kant, and neither has Rationalism.[126] But Lutheran theology can be grateful to him for freeing it from the onerous responsibility of proving by means of reason that which is known by faith through the givenness of God in the Cross of Jesus Christ. Thus, by proving "that all attempts to establish a theology by the aid of speculation alone are fruitless, that the principles of reason as applied to nature do not conduct to any theological truths, and, consequently, that a rational theology can have no existence," [127] Kant made possible a reconstruction of the subject matter and method of theology that could have cleared the way for a recovery of Luther's understanding of the nature of faith.

KANT ON TIME AND SPACE

Nor is this the only point of contact between Kant's epistemology and Lutheran theology. It was Kant who first systematized philosophically the insight mentioned earlier into the relationship between our spatial perception and reality as this had been adumbrated in Lutheran Christology.[128] In the Transcendental Aesthetic of the *Critique* he showed that space cannot be a property of objects as they are in themselves, but that both space and time are the necessary *a priori* forms of all phenomena, space being superimposed upon the phenomena of our external sense and time upon those of our internal sense.[129] The fact that my perception of an object is spatial does not mean that the thing-in-itself exists spatially. And though Kant does not himself indicate the connection between this discovery and the doctrines of the Person of Christ and of God, it is no less true that this is the necessary conclusion to be drawn from a serious consideration of the timelessness of God [130] as from the Lutheran doctrine that the presence of Christ is a reality without being spatially perceptible.

Closely related to this insight is the distinction which Kant drew between the empirical and the transcendental Ego.[131] In Luther's thought a similar distinction appears when he describes the Ego which receives the Gospel. It is necessary, Luther maintains, "dass du aus dir und von dir kommen moegest," [132] that is, that the Ego of experience be transcended in faith. Kant achieved the distinction, as Elert has pointed out,[133] by the reduction of consciousness to the *a priori* of the Ego and in this followed mysticism rather than Luther's theology. The results he achieved, however, were closer to Luther's understanding of self-consciousness than was the object-subject antithesis in which Orthodoxy had sought to express this relationship.

KANT'S MORAL PHILOSOPHY

As Lutheran theology influenced Kant's *Critique of Pure Reason,* so also the book he wrote as a sequel to the *Critique, Religion Within the Limits of Reason Alone,* bears the marks of the author's Christian, specifically Lutheran, background. The ethical precepts developed in this work are in many ways a secularized version of the Christianity which Kant had learned to know in its Lutheran form. A recent study of Kant's moral philosophy has tersely summarized the religious character of Kant's ethic: "The whole of Kant's moral philosophy might almost be described under the title of one of his last books as 'religion within the bounds of reason alone.' For him religion is primarily the Christian religion purified, not only from the dogmas of an authoritarian Church, but also from miracles and mysteries and from what he regards as the substitution of historical beliefs for rational ones. His Formula of Universal Law, insisting as it does on the spirit as opposed to the letter of the moral law, is his version of the Christian doctrine that we are saved by faith and not by works. His Formula of the End in Itself is his way of expressing the Christian view that every individual human being has a unique and infinite value and should be treated as such. His Formula of the Kingdom of Ends as a Kingdom of Nature is quite explicitly his rational form of recognising a church invisible and visible, the Kingdom of God which has to be made manifest on earth." [134]

The Calling

Kant's very definition of religion has a Lutheran cast, but the same secularization of Christian thought referred to above is present here, too. What he calls religion is "the recognition of all our duties as divine commands." [135] As an adequate description or definition of the experience of the Holy this certainly leaves much to be desired. [136] But it bears a striking resemblance to one of the most significant contributions of Lutheranism to Christian ethics, Luther's doctrine of the calling. [137] In opposition to the stratification of ethics in medieval Catholicism, Luther insisted that the humblest toil was as pleasing as the life of the intellect in the eyes of God. For Luther every occupation was a divine calling if it was carried on to the glory of God, and all the duties associated with that calling were to be regarded as divine commands. [138] Kant's Lutheranism made him think of all duties as divine commands, but his moralism made him understand this to be the essence of religion. In that connection various scholars have pointed out that the eternal validity of the moral law in Kant's theory is his version of the Christian doctrine of the eternity of God and of His will, [139] another example of the curious mingling of Christianity and moralism that permeates so much of his thought.

Radical Evil

There is one element in Kant's moral philosophy which, if consistently carried out, might have transformed him from the moralist that he was to the philosopher of Protestantism that he is sometimes claimed to be. [140] The element is his doctrine of the radical evil, also enunciated in his *Religion Within the Limits of Reason Alone,* though he devoted a separate article to the problem a year earlier. [141] The radical evil, Kant defines as that in human nature which "corrupts all maxims," accepting the postulates of the moral imperative, but perverting them into tools of self-aggrandizement and thus subverting the very basis of moral living. It was not reason alone that led him to this insight, but the Christian doctrine of man which underlies much of what a recent study has called Kant's "pre-critical ethics." [142] As Reinhold Niebuhr has observed, "in analyzing the human capacity for self-deception and its ability to make the worse appear the better reason for the sake of providing a moral façade for selfish actions, Kant penetrates into spiritual intricacies and mysteries to which he seems to remain completely blind in his *Critique of Practical Reason.*" [143] That Kant did not develop his understanding of the radical evil into a complete doctrine of man can be attributed to his moralistic pride, but that he stated it at all can be credited to his Lutheran training.

The philosophical revolution of Immanuel Kant destroyed the pride and the presumption with which the human reason had dared to pass upon the mysteries of God. It could therefore have been a real boon to a theology which had gone through a losing battle with philosophy. If the Lutheran theology of the nineteenth century had taken Kant's discoveries of the nature of knowledge and experience seriously, it could have set down a description of Christian doctrine in which the primacy of faith would have been asserted. Instead, much of Lutheran theology replaced Christian doctrine with a Kantian moralism. Those elements in Kant's system which could have been productive of genuine evangelical theology were shelved in favor of those which short-circuited Christian faith. Our study of Lutheranism and philosophy after Kant will trace that development in the nineteenth century and will seek to evaluate the new departure that came with the thought of Sören Kierkegaard.

5

The Nineteenth Century

In the person and thought of Immanuel Kant the rationalistic philosophy of the eighteenth century had produced its own destroyer. Using the tools with which the rationalism of Wolff had provided him, Kant proceeded to an analysis of the function of reason that subverted the foundations of rationalism in both philosophy and theology.

So important is the work of Kant that the history of nineteenth-century thought cannot be interpreted except against the background of the "Copernican revolution" which he effected.[1] This is true of nineteenth-century logic, epistemology, aesthetics, and ethics. But nowhere does this fact apply more directly than in the field of the philosophy of religion and in the theologies which were informed by that philosophy of religion.

It is just in those two areas — theology and philosophy of religion — that a curious ambivalence implicit in Kant becomes apparent, as we noted in the previous chapter. After the Kantian revolution, theology and philosophy could have gone in one of two directions. Whatever may have been Kant's own

intentions in the matter,[2] his delineation of the proper function
of reason in the understanding of reality, especially of religious
reality, could have provided nineteenth-century theology with
a weapon against the rationalism that had so debilitated Lutheranism in the preceding century. When the *Critique of Pure
Reason* showed that basic religious and metaphysical concepts
like God, freedom, and immortality cannot be reached by pure
reason,[3] it opened the way for a prophetic reassertion of the
Lutheran understanding of faith. Over against the smugness
and ease with which rationalistic theology had claimed to be
able to examine basic religious affirmations, Kant's *Critique*
declared, once for all, that these affirmations can be either
accepted or denied on the basis of pure reason. He thus
dealt a deathblow to the rationalistic speculations of seventeenth-century Orthodoxy and to its basically Aristotelian philosophical framework. His *Critique* was equally destructive to
the rationalistic repudiation of Orthodoxy which we have
sketched in our earlier discussion. Thus Kant did not take one
side or the other in the conflict between Orthodox rationalism
and anti-Orthodox rationalism. His *Critique of Pure Reason*
declared the conflict as such to be illegitimate, since underlying
the positions of both antagonists was a false faith in the powers
of reason to come to grips with the realities of religion.

FAITH AND KANT'S CRITICISM

How this discovery could have benefited theology is evident
from the tension we have described between Luther and Melanchthon in the definition of faith.[4] Kant's criticism does no
harm to Luther's view of faith. For Luther did not accept
Christ as his Lord on the basis of rational evidence or proof.
Rather He was there as a real and concrete Person, as the

sovereign Lord of nature and of history. Luther's personal experience of God was too vivid and too intense for him to concern himself with the question of whether reason can prove Him to be real. In contrast to this stands Melanchthon's intellectualism, for which the constructs and discoveries of the reason were important factors in the religious life. It was their function to provide the mind with certainty about the validity of Christian doctrine and to weave that doctrine into a comprehensive whole. If Kant's criticisms are applied to Melanchthon's theological and philosophical structure, the entire basis of that structure collapses. Because much of eighteenth-century theology was still traveling on Melanchthonian presuppositions, it was seriously threatened by Kant. This should have meant a reorientation of the task and content of theology by new reference to the centrality of faith rather than of reason in theological thought.

THEOLOGY AFTER KANT

Anyone who knows the history of the theology of the nineteenth century will realize that things did not work out that way. Instead of reorienting the task of theology in the direction of faith, the nineteenth century recast theology in terms of experience and morality. It diluted the content of Christian faith until little remained but a vague conception of God, a humanized picture of Christ, and an ethic scarcely distinguishable from the "prudential virtues"[5] of the respectable and rational pagan. And it did this on the basis of Kant's philosophy. After Kant had declared the content of Christian faith to be unattainable in rational terms, much of Lutheran theology came to believe that therefore that content was unimportant. As we shall see, this was the tack taken by many outstanding Lutheran theologians in the nineteenth century. Thus Kant's philosophy, which could have provided theology with a new understanding of its essential responsibility, became instead the root of an unevangelical moralism.

The metaphysical implications of Kant's thought, however, were not neglected in the nineteenth century. They were taken up and developed into an advanced metaphysical system by German Idealism.[6] Through the researches of Wilhelm Luetgert[7] and Richard Kroner[8] we have come to understand this movement more fully as an important chapter in the history of culture and particularly in the history of religious philosophy. It is, in fact, the chief area in which Lutheranism and philosophy interacted upon each other during the nineteenth century. Nineteenth-century German Idealism — or spiritualism, to use a more appropriate name[9] — is made up of a variegated and confusing group of thinkers whose speculations form one of the most complicated chapters in the history of ideas.[10] We cannot here devote attention to the minute details of their respective systems. But underlying these systems are several basic religious and philosophical presuppositions and problems.

Materialism and Mechanism

No single factor is more responsible for the development of German Idealism than the prevalence of materialism in the eighteenth and nineteenth centuries.[11] We have already noted the movements of thought in England and France during the seventeenth and eighteenth centuries and their implication for the Church.[12] Materialism was the logical consequent of those movements. Added to the skeptical bent of Deism and French agnosticism was the impact of the natural sciences upon religious and philosophical thought.[13] The mechanical world projected by Isaac Newton and his disciples became the basis for a world view that sought to explain everything, even the mind, on materialistic grounds. Though all the advocates of materialism did not go as far in their views as Paul Heinrich von Holbach, his *Systeme de la Nature* may be taken as a fair sample of advanced materialism.[14] By a combination of logic and sarcasm Holbach cast doubt upon all the tenets of Christianity and produced a system in which the soul and the mind had no place. It was in opposition to such materialism that German Idealism developed its emphasis upon the spirit both in man and in the universe. The problem of the continuity between the Ego and the world, which Kant had raised but had not satisfactorily solved,[15] gave Idealism the opportunity it needed to assert the primacy of the spirit. Over against materialism, which taught that what I share with the world is the stuff of which my body is made, Idealism sought both the principle of existence and the principle of thought in *Geist,* a term for which the English word "spirit" is at best an inadequate translation.[16]

THE PRIMACY OF "GEIST"

As disciples of Kant, the Idealists could not completely ignore the sciences; for Kant himself had come to metaphysics through physics.[17] What they repudiated was the attempt on the part of materialism to employ the methods and results of the sciences in the determination of philosophical and ethical values. The desire to affirm the primacy of *Geist* in human life is Idealism's answer to that attempt. Materialism and Idealism share an essentially monistic world view: both sought one unifying principle in man and in the universe by which all the phenomena of nature as well as of consciousness could be explained.[18] But in identifying that unifying principle, Idealism allied itself with the Romanticism current at the time, especially in Germany, to defend the spirit against the flesh.[19]

The process by which monistic Idealism arrives at its synthesis has perhaps never been more trenchantly analyzed than by William James. "First, there is a healthy faith that the world must be rational and self-consistent. . . . Next, we find a loyal clinging to the rationalist belief that sense-data and their associations are incoherent, and that only in substituting a conceptual order for their order can truth be found. Third, the substituted conceptions are treated intellectualistically, that is, as mutually exclusive and discontinuous, so that the first innocent continuity of the flow of sense-experience is shattered for us without any higher conceptual continuity taking its place. Finally, since this broken state of things is intolerable, the absolute *deus ex machina* is called on to mend it in his own way, since we cannot mend it in ours."[20]

When applied to the area of religion, such an approach was bound to have serious consequences. Its desire for a single unifying principle and its concern with the Absolute meant that it had to reject the dualism implicit in the Christian doctrine of God as Creator[21] in favor of a depersonalized God whose difference from the world is at best one of degree rather than of kind. As we shall see, it was no accident that some Idealists produced views closely related to the pantheism of Bruno and Spinoza. Similarly, Idealism's commitment to *Geist* made it impossible for its adherents to take the Incarnation seriously; in spite of the fact that the philosophy of history was one of their chief concerns, they tended to see history as the unfolding of the world spirit rather than as the arena for God's condescension in Christ.[22] All of this is not to minimize the stupendous literary and philosophical achievements of Idealism. But when viewed in terms of its implications for and influence on theology, Idealism must be seen as a circumvention of important areas of Christian faith.

LUTHERANISM AND IDEALISM

The problem of the relationship between Lutheran theology and Idealism [23] becomes all the more curious in view of the fact that the three outstanding philosophical leaders of Idealism —Fichte, Schelling, and Hegel — were all trained in Lutheran theology. No history of the interrelations between Lutheranism and philosophy would be adequate without at least a brief examination of those three thinkers.

Johann Gottlieb Fichte [24] studied Lutheran theology at the universities of Jena and Leipzig, but by temperament and inclination he was more a philosopher than a theologian. His earliest philosophical impulses seem to have come from Spinoza, by whose metaphysics he was deeply stirred.[25] It was apparently not until after he had completed his formal education that he became acquainted with the work of Kant, whom he later also learned to know personally.[26] The Kantian philosophy may, however, be regarded as the principal contributing factor in the formation of Fichte's philosophy of religion.

FICHTE AND KANT

The earliest articulation of that philsophy of religion appeared, when Fichte was thirty years old, under the title *Critique of All Revelation*.[27] So pronounced was the influence of the critcial philosophy on the anonymous work, an influence apparent even in the title, that many contemporaries regarded it as Kant's own composition.[28] Here Kant's definition of religion

as a recognition of all our duties as divine commands [29] comes
to full fruition. Fichte begins by positing the existence of an
internally implanted moral law in all men. But most men seek
a validation for this moral law outside themselves, regarding
the inner testimony of their moral consciousness as untrust-
worthy. This validation they profess to find in a legislating
Deity, who imposes His will upon men. Religion is, then,
nothing more than an elaborate attempt to root the validity
of the moral law in a supposed God — an attempt which may
be unnecessary philosophically, since the moral law is internal
to begin with, but which is necessary nonetheless simply because most people believe it to be necessary.[30]

Fichte's later works on the philosophy of religion reveal that
although he never transcended the moralism of his earlier
thought, he did relate his philosophy of religion to a rather
carefully thought out metaphysical system. The striving for the
Absolute and the monism which we have seen as marks of
Idealism become apparent in these later works, especially in
Fichte's treatise on *The Vocation of Man*.[31] By definition the
Absolute must be thought of as infinite; hence we cannot ascribe
personality to God, for personality denotes limitation.[32] Nor
dare we identify the Absolute with substance,[33] for this is to
conceive of God spatially. It is vain to seek the Absolute outside ourselves, when there is something about us which is infinite, absolute, and abiding. This is the moral law, which
binds together all the phenomena of experience in a meaningful whole. And since the moral order is both infinite and sure,
it is God.[34] The freedom to realize and express myself in
accordance with this moral order, this God, is the cornerstone
of what has aptly been termed Fichte's "ethical pantheism." [35]

FICHTE'S ETHICAL PANTHEISM

To establish this view of God, the treatise moves from the doubt that comes when I realize that my understanding of the world is false, through the knowledge that makes me look into myself rather than into the world for truth, to the faith that assures me of the reality of those values which give purpose to my life.[36] There is, then, no God in the traditional Christian sense of the Father of our Lord Jesus Christ; the moral order is God, and both the external world and human consciousness are to be explained by reference to this moral order. The depersonalization of God to which we have previously called attention [37] and the moralization and secularization of religion which we have seen in Kant [38] are continued in Fichte's philosophy.

As a matter of fact, Fichte's system denies validity not only to the objective existence of God, but even to my experience of the external world. Proceeding, as it does, from an egocentric bias, his metaphysic casts doubt upon the most elementary of empirical data and makes science useless and irrelevant.[39] It was the intention of Fichte's disciple and later opponent, Friedrich Wilhelm Schelling, to repair this inadequacy.[40] With the vagaries of Schelling's development we cannot be concerned in this context, for they are many and devious.[41]

SCHELLING'S VIEW OF GOD

In at least one respect, however, Schelling is important for the history of the interrelations between Lutheranism and philosophy. Himself a product of Lutheran theological study,[42] he wanted to construct a metaphysic and a philosophy of religion in which the valid claims of all fields of human endeavor would have a place. He sought a comprehensive system,[43] and this in part accounts for the complexity of the ideas he produced. Desiring to make up for the onesidedness of Fichte's emphasis upon the consciousness, Schelling developed an idea of God that bears much affinity to Spinoza's pantheism.[44] Schelling's God is not, like Fichte's, merely the projection of the inner moral law. He is the force that binds the universe together, the *Weltgeist,* to use Hegel's term, by whom both nature and history are guided and permeated.[45] Since, according to Schelling, nature is existing reason,[46] his theism, which does not distinguish between God and the universe, is as depersonalized as that of Fichte, which does not distinguish between God and the inner moral law. But by dealing with the problem of history in connection with his idea of God,[47] Schelling asked the question which Hegel was later to answer. In many ways, Schelling belongs more to the history of Gnostic speculation, together with Nicholas of Cusa, Giordano Bruno, and Jakob Boehme, than he does to the history of philosophy.[48] Nevertheless, he did seek to relate his doctrine of God to a theology of history, and he is not the only thinker in history who is more important for the questions he asked than for the answers he gave.

Important for both his questions and his answers, as well as for our problem, is the last of the three thinkers mentioned above, Georg Wilhelm Friedrich Hegel.[49] It is only through the recent translation of the young Hegel's works on theology that the English-speaking public has been able to appreciate more fully the deeply theological tenor of his thought.[50] In the words of Kroner, "Hegel's philosophy is in itself a speculative religion — Christianity spelt by dialectic." [51]

HEGEL ON THE RELIGION OF JESUS

The conflict involved in such a speculative consideration of Christianity is apparent from Hegel's entire early life, so penetratingly sketched by Wilhelm Dilthey.[52] It comes into prominence in the essay on *The Positivity of the Christian Religion,* which Hegel wrote in his later twenties.[53] In a manner that presaged of the Hegelian theologians who were to follow,[54] Hegel takes up the problem of the relation of Jesus to the early beginnings of the Church. Careful consideration brings him to the conclusion that the religion of Jesus was essentially ethical in its orientation. Throughout the essay, and especially in the first part, the influence of Kant's moralism is apparent.[55] The ethical religion of Jesus was replaced, according to Hegel, by the "positive," i. e., dogmatic religion of the Church, which refused to set men free morally but chose to hedge them in with dogma and authority instead.[56] In the essay on *The Spirit of Christianity,* written shortly after the first part of the *Positivity,* Hegel emerges as a more independent thinker.[57] Also dealing with the problem of the teachings of Jesus, the later discussion contains a lengthy analysis and critique of Kant's theories of morality in the light of the religious ethic of Jesus.[58] Hegel finds that Kant's emphasis upon duty and upon the domination of reason over inclination is contrary to the spirit of Jesus, who taught that only that deed is good which is freely performed.

By interpreting Jesus as essentially a teacher of morality, however, Hegel showed his inclination to secularize Christian teachings and change them into abstract moral principles. In his later development he went far beyond these early attempts of his youth, but the secularization remains. The distinctive feature of Hegel's maturer productions is the fact that not only the ethics, but also the metaphysics of Christianity had to be reduced to a set of principles not derived from faith but from speculation. There is much to be said in favor of the view that in Hegel the secularization of Lutheran theology described above [59] becomes virtually complete.

THE TRINITY IN HEGEL

Abundant evidence for such an interpretation is furnished by Hegel's doctrine of God. [60] He refused to content himself with the shallow theologies of Kant and Fichte, [61] and though he was at first drawn to Schelling's nature philosophy, [62] he eventually found that, too, inadequate for his needs. [63] The god of Hegel is more than the validation of our moral consciousness, though he is that. [64] On the other hand, he cannot be naively identified with world process, as Schelling was inclined to think. [65] He must be both immanent and transcendent — immanent enough to affect the world, transcendent enough to direct the world. [66] The right synthesis of immanence and transcendence Hegel found in the Christian doctrine of the Trinity as he reinterpreted it. [67] By its teaching of the Trinity, Christianity seemed to him to have made room for God's activity in history without sacrificing His lordship over history. Hegel's monumental *Philosophy of History* is a colossal attempt to formulate this new Trinitarian synthesis. [68] God is the world spirit who is accomplishing his purposes in history, he is the Reason guiding history, as, according to Hegel, the prologue of John's Gospel teaches. [69] Amid the confusing theories of his *Phenomenology of Mind* this stands out clearly: God is the Absolute, the ever-present, but ever-evasive object of the human search. [70]

But the Absolute does not attain self-realization except in

man. The world spirit becomes incarnate over and over again as man's search for truth progresses. This progress does not proceed statically; it is a dynamic process of thesis, antithesis, synthesis, by which systems die and in dying live on in their successors.[71] Goethe's "Stirb und werde" epitomizes that paradox,[72] even in God. Christ had to die to attain God's purpose, for that is the rule of all of life.

Students of theology will recognize this as a dehydrated version of basic Christian beliefs. What is taken in Christianity as having happened once for all in Christ[73] — incarnation, revelation, crucifixion, resurrection — is generalized into the pattern of all nature and history. And Christianity is made into a natural religion in spite of Hegel's emphasis upon revelation. Idealism emerges in Hegel, then, as an emancipated theology, no longer requiring the unique act of God in Jesus Christ for its validation. The process of secularization, begun by the Rationalists and continued by Kant and Fichte, is fulfilled in Hegel. Theology remains the queen of the sciences, but the queen is an impostor.

THEOLOGY AFTER HEGEL

In the midst of such a process of secularization, theology, as it had been previously understood, lost its *raison d'être*. Hegelian philosophy felt able to penetrate to ultimate truth concerning God, the universe, and the meaning of history. There was really very little left for theology to do. The only alternatives seemed to be either to submit to Hegelianism or to assert a new definition of religion to which neither Kant's critiques nor Hegel's speculations applied. The former course was taken by the Hegelian theologians, whom we shall describe briefly later. The latter alternative was the one chosen by the most influential

Protestant thinker of the nineteenth century, Friedrich Daniel Ernst Schleiermacher.[74]

The Orthodox and the Rationalist views of religion were agreed in maintaining that the substance of religion is something to be known, that religion consists in knowledge.[75] Against both of them Kant and the Idealists urged the view that the truths of theology are beyond the reach of sure knowledge, and that therefore the essence of religion lies in morality. This is the background against which the work of Schleiermacher should be interpreted. He found himself unable to identify religion either with intellectual knowledge or with morality. In place of these definitions he advanced the theory that the constitutive feature of religion is feeling, that, specifically, religion is a "feeling of dependence." [76]

Within the brief compass of this study and of its restricted purpose we cannot go into Schleiermacher's system as such. The controversies that have raged over his significance are sufficient testimony to the power and originality of his genius.[77] For our purposes the most important aspects of Schleiermacher's work are the philosophical origins of his thought and their influence on his attempt to reinstate theology as a legitimate and respectable field of study.

The Influence of Romanticism

Perhaps the chief influence upon Schleiermacher's definition of religion as a feeling of dependence is German Romanticism.[78] In opposition to both sterile intellectualism and shallow moralism, the Romanticists in Germany as well as in England aimed to elevate feeling into a dominant place in literature and philosophy.[79] Taking his cue from the romanticism of his friends and associates, Schleiermacher saw in a romantic reinterpretation of the religious consciousness an opportunity to rescue religion from intellectualist criticism and moralist perversion.

The romantic proclivities thus acquired from his environment were confirmed by Schleiermacher's philosophical studies. Schleiermacher was one of the founders of modern Plato scholarship, a field in which he can still be studied with profit.[80] Steeped as he was in Platonic epistemology, he found it easy to fit his understanding of religion into the aesthetic idealism of Plato.[81] Spinoza, too, exerted an influence upon him.[82] Whatever may be its theological and philosophical fallacies,[83] it must be admitted that Spinoza's pantheism was intensely pious and deeply religious. Spinoza was so aware of the active presence of God permeating all things that he adored his "natura naturans"[84] with religious ardor. This approach evoked a ready response in Schleiermacher, and his doctrine of God shows a marked resemblance to that of Spinoza. As is the case with most of the thinkers of the nineteenth century, Kant also helped to make Schleiermacher what he was, though the influence was certainly more negative than positive.[85] Kant made it impossible for Schleiermacher — or for any other theologian, for that matter — to make the claims for the intellect which had been made by classical Protestant dogmatics. He thus forced Schleiermacher to look elsewhere than to the intellect for the validation of his religious beliefs.

PHILOSOPHY AND THEOLOGY IN SCHLEIERMACHER

And so it was that even when theology attempted to reassert itself against the tyranny of philosophy, its very reassertion was conditioned by philosophical thinking. Schleiermacher's subjectivism is a product of the philosophical tradition in which he stood. It is a supreme irony that what began as a defense of religion and theology against philosophy should have ended as little more than a battle between two philosophical systems. Theology still could not declare its independence from philosophy.

Even less independent of philosophy than Schleiermacher is the avowedly Hegelian theology of many Lutheran theologians in the nineteenth century. Of particular interest is the Hegelian derivation of German New Testament scholarship.[86] Hegel's philosophy of history was found to be very fruitful in the interpretation of the history of the Early Church. David Friedrich Strauss' *Life of Jesus* tried to explain the primitive impulse of Jesus and the establishment of the Church in terms of Hegel's historical speculations.[87] An entire school of New Testament study, the Tuebingen school of Baur,[88] gave the impetus to much of contemporary scholarship in Biblical studies and church history by its use of Hegel's philosophy for theological research. The impact of Hegel upon nineteenth-century Lutheran theology was not restricted to Germany, however. In at least two other sections of the Lutheran Church, Scandinavia and Slovakia, Hegel's influence appears. Among the Scandinavians, Bishop Hans Martensen of Denmark stands out as a prominent example of the synthesis between Hegelianism and Lutheranism;[89] as we shall see, it was against this synthesis that Kierkegaard was to protest. In Slovakia, Hegel provided the dialectical framework for the ideological leaders of Slovak nationalism, and in the process it led them to a theological reconstruction as well.[90] Throughout most of Lutheran theology during the nineteenth century, Hegel's theories succeeded in destroying a considerable portion of Christian thought and in replacing it with abstract philosophical principles.

THE DILEMMA OF THEOLOGY

This was the dilemma of nineteenth-century Lutheran theology. In the development from Kant to Hegel, philosophy of religion had almost completely taken the place of theology, and the theological faculties were dominated by philosophical speculation. But the tragic aspect of the situation lay in the fact that a repristination of classical Lutheran Orthodoxy was impossible after Kant; he had destroyed the epistemological presuppositions upon which Orthodoxy had built its system. For that reason the attempts that were made to repristinate Orthodoxy failed to produce a lasting theology. The only way that evangelical theology would be able to reassert itself was by developing a new philosophy to counter the various blends of Kantianism, Hegelianism, and Spinozism that had crowded out the Christian theological witness.

THE PHILOSOPHY OF KIERKEGAARD

But if the new philosophy was to do more than to give up one speculative system in favor of another, it had to be related to the basic structure of Lutheran theology and rooted in faith.[91] The only philosophical framework in which Lutheran theology could be recast had to be a framework derived from that theology itself. It is this circumstance that gives meaning and relevance to the philosophy of Sören Kierkegaard. Kierkegaard is the first Christian philosopher to develop a critical philosophy in the truest and most complete sense of the word. He is, therefore, the climax of the development we have traced in this study. In him Lutheranism produced a philosopher whose thought has brought on a revolution in both theology and philosophy. But the revolution has made possible a recovery of the deep evangelical insights of the theology of Martin Luther.[92]

In the course of his development, Kierkegaard directed his criticism against all three of the movements we have sketched in nineteenth-century philosophy of religion — intellectualism, moralism, and aestheticism. The first was represented by the Hegelians, the second by the Kantians, the third by Schleiermacher.

Because it was Hegelian intellectualism which had infected the Danish Church and Danish theology,[93] Kierkegaard's sharpest criticism was directed against Hegelianism.[94] Despite the debt he owed to Hegel,[95] the Danish thinker poured out his scorn upon what he usually terms "the System," [96] referring to Hegel and Martensen. One of the most important of his works is his *Concluding Unscientific Postscript,* which called into question the basic premises of intellectualism, particularly the Hegelian version.[97] Intellectualism claims to have domesticated the truth and to have fitted it perfectly into its preconceived patterns. But it has not yet learned to exist! By its supposedly dispassionate analysis of the "objective" truth, external to all experience, it has completely perverted the truth.[98] For truth is not a something with which I may deal as I choose, as though it were outside me. Truth is always personal, subjective. It comes in involvement, and it is hard to live with.[99] The Hegelian assumption that a neatly balanced system of reality can be constructed rationally from the truth is a tragic delusion. Only that is true which is true for me.

EXISTENTIALISM

In our first chapter we pointed to the affinities between this existential understanding of truth and Luther's theology.[100]

When viewed in contrast to the development of Lutheranism and philosophy between Luther and Kierkegaard, those affinities become all the more striking. Melanchthonianism, Orthodoxy, Rationalism, and Hegelianism all sought a comprehensive rational system. To that extent they all constitute a misinterpretation of Luther. And although the existential insight was never lost in the religiousness of the Lutheran Church,[101] Kierkegaard is the first major thinker after Luther to build it into a working and critical philosophy.

There had been others, as we have seen, who repudiated intellectualism. But in its place they had proposed either moralism or aestheticism. Kierkegaard rejects these viewpoints, too. His critique of moralism is expressed in some of the most profound sections of his works.[102] The story of the faith of Abraham haunted Kierkegaard because of its moral implications.[103] Abraham had been promised that in his Seed all the nations of the earth would be blessed and had received the revelation of God's will forbidding the taking of human life. He had, therefore, both a religion and a morality. But the very same God from whom both the promise and the prohibition had come now ordered him to perform an act in complete violation of both — the sacrifice of his son Isaac. By this act God's purposes would be frustrated and His moral commandment disobeyed. Considering the struggle through which Abraham passed, Kierkegaard puts the problem in philosophical terms: "Is there a teleological suspension of the ethical?"[104] That is, can the moral law be set aside on the basis of a personal, existential encounter with God? Or is the Moral Law so eternal and so inviolable, as Kant and Fichte had supposed, that no such encounter could be either valid or binding?

TELEOLOGICAL SUSPENSION OF THE ETHICAL

The decision which Abraham made indicated to Kierkegaard where the answer lies. Abraham did not balance the claim of God upon his heart against the claims of an abstract set of ethical principles. God was the sovereign Lord, not bound by any set of principles or laws. His demands and commands have priority over any such principles or laws. And so there is indeed a teleological suspension of the ethical — when the *telos* involved is the God who is the Father of our Lord Jesus Christ. What Kierkegaard presents here is a Lutheran denunciation of the moralism which had replaced God with a moral law. The faith of Luther and of Kierkegaard rules out any moralistic view of God's person and action. Moralism is no better than intellectualism as the basis for a Christian philosophy.

With much of this, Schleiermacher would have agreed; and, despite Brunner's insistence to the contrary,[105] Schleiermacher and Kierkegaard do have much in common.[106] They are especially close in their negative development over against intellectualism and moralism. It is significant that throughout his life Kierkegaard struggled to overcome a romanticist interpretation of religion. The longest of his works, *Either/Or,* is a moving personal document recording the course of that struggle and his ultimate victory over an aesthetic world view.[107]

KIERKEGAARD'S AESTHETICISM

Kierkegaard was a poetic soul, with deep artistic and musical sensitivities.[108] He was attracted by the prospect of developing a dainty and wistful Christianity in which the Beautiful and the Holy could be fused into a single value. Rudolf Otto has shown the many points of correspondence between these two, but in his discussion of Schleiermacher he has also indicated the weaknesses of such a fusion.[109] Similarly, but with far more prophetic insight and self-denunciation, Kierkegaard forced himself to pass through what he terms "the aesthetic stage" to the religious stage.[110] Life's tragedy and its pain were not for Kierkegaard, as they are for religious romanticism, ancient and modern,[111] a part of the birth pangs of the Eternal. He refused to see in suffering and in death something to be endured for the sake of the Good and the Beautiful which will inevitably issue from them. *Angst* was too much of an existential, God-centered reality for him to flirt with naturalist, aesthetic notions.[112] Ever since his father had cursed God on the plains of Jutland,[113] Kierkegaard had known the loneliness and the dread that comes when a man is forsaken by God. There is nothing beautiful about *Angst,* and I can never know or predict its outcome. A romanticist Kierkegaard was, but it is a tribute to his faithful pursuit of the question "What does it mean to be Christian?" that he transcended the romanticism that lay so close to 'his heart and came to the Christian interpretation of human existence.

Parallels to Luther in this viewpoint immediately suggest themselves. He was also temperamentally attracted to an aesthetic outlook on life.[114] But, like Kierkegaard, he transcended it in the name of the Gospel. No theory of "the creativity of God"[115] in nature, art, and society would have satisfied him. In his experience of the *Deus absconditus* he had become too aware of what might be termed "the destructivity of God" to see God as anything else but the Lord. By overcoming the aesthetic interpretation of religion, Kierkegaard made possible a new insight into this aspect of Luther's theology, too.

KIERKEGAARD'S SIGNIFICANCE FOR THEOLOGY

From what has been said here, as well as in our first chapter, we can draw the conclusion that the existential philosophy of Sören Kierkegaard performed a great service toward a solution of the problem of a philosophy for Lutheran theology. The many affinities between his point of view and Luther's theology suggest that contemporary Lutheran theology could do much worse than to look more deeply into Kierkegaard for the categories in which to articulate its faith. This is not to say that theology can accept him uncritically; his opposition to "systems" and "schools" would make such uncritical acceptance a violation of his own ideas.[116] There are several blind spots in his thought, notably the individualism and subjectivism which have prevented most of his followers from articulating an adequate doctrine of the Church.[117] But when compared with the other philosophies to which Lutheran theology has been linked, Kierkegaard's philosophy has much to say to Lutheran theology.

This is the story of the interrelations between Lutheranism and philosophy from Luther to Kierkegaard. There are many problems and men whom space did not permit us to treat, and those we did examine were of necessity accorded brief treatment. But this study would make itself liable to the charge of historicism if we did not add at least a word on the significance of this material for the present theological and philosophical crisis.

From what has been said in these five chapters the interdependence of theology and philosophy in the history of Lutheranism is clear. From this interdependence it follows, however, that we should be guilty of utter self-deception if we were to maintain that we or our contemporaries are free of any involvement in philosophy merely because we wish we were or because we think we ought to be. As long as it is necessary or advisable for theologians to witness to their faith in a systematic manner, as long as the Christian Church is interested in relating itself positively to the problems of civilization and culture, so long theology will need philosophy.

A PHILOSOPHY FOR LUTHERANISM?

The question naturally arises: What philosophy? Negatively speaking, it certainly dare not be the philosophy that was current in the Age of Orthodoxy. In spite of the religious and theological value of the doctrinal formulations of the seventeenth century, the philosophical framework of reference which shaped those formulations cannot be uncritically accepted. We may think theologically as though Schleiermacher had never lived, and much of American Lutheranism does. But we may not think philosophically as though Kant had never lived. There is no going behind the critical philosophy and its validated results. Lutheranism dare not imitate the obscurantism of Neo-Thomism, for which the work of Kant is still *terra incognita.*

And yet Kant cannot be the philosopher of Lutheranism. We have seen the religious inadequacy of Kant's ethics and metaphysics. Rather, if Lutheranism and philosophy are to come to terms to their mutual advantage, we shall need a new philosophy. The work of Kierkegaard is a beginning, but much remains to be done, especially in cosmology, for the construction of a Lutheran philosophy. Such a philosophy will have to be worked out with constant reference to the tenets of Christianity as we know them in their Lutheran description. But it dare not bow to a heteronomous theologism. It must develop on its own grounds and in terms of its own canons. The Lutheran doctrines of the universal priesthood of believers and of the value of all vocations in the sight of God certainly hold in the case of the Christian philosopher, too. Like the calling of the Christian ruler, the Christian father, and the Christian theologian, the work of the Christian philosopher must also be carried on *coram Deo*. But if thus carried on and if kept in constant touch with the Gospel, it can be a good work and pleasing to God.

It is not the primary task of the Christian Church to develop philosophies. The responsibility of the Christian Church is to witness to the forgiveness of sins and the lordship of Christ. But that lordship exerts itself over the total life of the total man and therefore over his mind, too. If Jesus Christ is truly the Lord, then the intellect, too, must serve Him. It will perform this service if it takes up the task of working out a Christian philosophy. It is to be hoped that twentieth-century Lutheranism may produce Christian thinkers of the ability and consecration necessary for that task.

NOTES

NOTES TO CHAPTER I

[1] Emil Brunner, *Revelation and Reason*, translated by Olive Wyon (Philadelphia, 1946), pp. 389—390.

[2] Karl Holl, "Luthers Urteile ueber sich selbst," *Gesammelte Aufsaetze zur Kirchengeschichte*, I, *Luther* (7th ed.; Tuebingen, 1948), pp. 406—407 for some representative quotations on this contrast.

[3] Theses 19—21 of the "Disputatio Heidelbergae habita" (1518) in *D. Martin Luthers Werke* (Weimar, 1883 ff.; henceforth abbreviated as *WA*), I, 354. Cf. Edward Ellwein, "Die Entfaltung der Theologia crucis in Luthers Hebraeerbriefvorlesung" in *Theologische Aufsaetze, Karl Barth zum 50. Geburtstag* (Muenchen, 1936), pp. 382—404.

[4] Etienne Gilson, *L'Esprit de la philosophie médiévale* (2nd ed.; Paris, 1944), pp. 1—38, 110—132.

[5] Alfred North Whitehead, *Process and Reality* (New York, 1929), p. 53.

[6] Cf. Charles Norris Cochrane, *Christianity and Classical Culture* (New York, 1944), pp. 222—232; Cochrane's entire brilliant analysis is relevant to our problem.

[7] Anders Nygren, *Agape and Eros, A Study of the Christian Idea of Love*, translated by A. G. Hebert and Philip S. Watson, II, Part II (London, 1939), p. 232 ff. and *passim* through most of Part II.

[8] Etienne Gilson, *Christianity and Philosophy*, translated by Ralph MacDonald (New York, 1939), esp. pp. 76—81 and the entire chapter on "Theology and Philosophy," pp. 82—102.

[9] Cf. G. Bauch, "Wittenberg und die Scholastik," *Neues Archiv fuer saechsische Geschichte*, XVIII (1897), p. 285 ff. on Luther's opportunities for learning to know the scholastics.

121

[10] This does not apply, of course, to Peter Lombard, on whose *Sententiae* Luther lectured 1510—1511; his comments on the Lombard, important for his early development, appear *WA* IX, 29—94; cf. the remarks of Otto Scheel, *Martin Luther. Vom Katholizismus zur Reformation*, II, *Im Kloster* (Tuebingen, 1917), pp. 210—248; on his attitude toward philosophy, see p. 232 ff., with the accompanying notes.

[11] On Luther's appraisal of the scholastics, see the ironic comments of Otto Scheel, *op. cit.*, p. 356, note 32.

[12] Cf. my essay "The Structure of Luther's Piety," *Una Sancta* (Martinmas, 1947), p. 19, notes 43—46 for references to the primary and secondary literature on this question.

[13] Maurice De Wulf, *History of Medieval Philosophy*, translated by Ernest C. Messenger, II (New York, 1926), pp. 245—250, for a trenchant summary.

[14] Cf. in general, Heinrich Boehmer, *Road to Reformation*, translated by John W. Doberstein and Theodore G. Tappert (Philadelphia, 1946), pp. 22—31.

[15] Anatole France, *The Garden of Epicurus*, quoted in John Herman Randall, *The Making of the Modern Mind* (revised edition, Boston, 1940), p. 17.

[16] Otto Scheel, "Zum wissenschaftlichen Weltbild Luthers" in *Geschichtliche Studien, Albert Hauck zum 70. Geburtstag dargebracht* (Leipzig, 1916), pp. 220—234. See also the scintillating discussion by Heinrich Bornkamm, *Luther und das Naturbild der Neuzeit* (Berlin, 1937).

[17] "Occam, mein lieber Meister," *WA* XXX-2, 300; ". . . magister meus," *WA, Tischreden* (henceforth abbreviated as *Ti*), II, 516.

[18] Reinhold Seeberg, *Die religioesen Grundgedanken des jungen Luthers und ihr Verhaeltnis zum Ockamismus und der deutschen Mystik*, Vol. VI of "Greifswalder Studien zur Lutherforschung und neuzeitlichen Geistesgeschichte" (Berlin und Leipzig, 1931).

[19] In his preface to Volume II of the Wittenberg edition of Luther's works, *Corpus Reformatorum* (henceforth abbreviated as *CR*), VI, 155—170, Melanchthon enumerates the theological and philosophical influences upon the young Luther.

[20] See the brief but precise discussion by M. Reu, *Luther's German Bible* (Columbus, 1934), pp. 288—289, note 14.

[21] Cf. the detailed exposition of Lynn Thorndike, *Science and Thought in the Fifteenth Century* (New York, 1929), and the immense amount of material on Renaissance superstition in his *History of Magic and Experimental Science*, III—IV (New York, 1934). On the general character of the philosophy of the Italian Renaissance, see the comments of John Addington Symonds, *Renaissance in Italy* (Modern Library Edition; New York, n. d.), II, pp. 411—442.

[22] Walter Pater, *The Renaissance* (New York, 1919), pp. 24—40. More recent scholarship on the thought of Ficino is the work of Paul Oskar Kristeller, *The Philosophy of Marsilio Ficino* (New York, 1943), and on Pico the essay of Ernst Cassirer, "Giovanni Pico della Mirandola," *Journal of the History of Ideas,* III (1942), pp. 123—144, 319—346. For representative essays by the two men see Ernst Cassirer and others (ed.), *The Renaissance Philosophy of Man* (Chicago, 1948), pp. 193—212, 223—254.

[23] On Gemisthus and Bessarion and their influence, see the work of Fr. Schulze, *Geschichte der philosophischen Renaissance,* I (Jena, 1874).

[24] See the pregnant discussion of Carl Neumann, "Byzantinische Kultur und Renaissancekultur," *Historische Zeitschrift,* XCI (1903), pp. 215—232, discussing some of these relationships.

[25] *The Civilization of the Renaissance in Italy* (London, 1944), esp. pp. 303—313.

[26] Paul Oskar Kristeller, "Florentine Platonism and Its Relations with Humanism and Scholasticism," *Church History,* VIII (1939), p. 201 ff.

[27] Fr. Seebohm, *The Oxford Reformers of 1498* (2nd ed.; London, 1869), is an attempt by a Reformation historian to evaluate the interactions of Colet and Erasmus. A recent Roman Catholic panegyric on Thomas More has tried to play down both the pagan elements of the Renaissance and the influence of Colet upon Protestantism: Theodore Maynard, *Humanist as Hero. The Life of Sir Thomas More* (New York, 1947), pp. 41—44.

[28] For a brief account of the revival of the classics in the sixteenth century, see Preserved Smith, *Age of the Reformation* (New York, 1920), pp. 574—578.

[29] A W. Hunzinger, *Lutherstudien,* I, *Luthers Neuplatonismus in der Psalmenvorlesung von 1513—1516* (Leipzig, 1906); cf. the thirty-sixth of the Heidelberg theses of 1518, *WA* I, 355.

[30] For example, "Enarratio in Genesin," *WA* XLII, 4; also *ibid., WA* XLII, 35.

[31] This oversimplification is developed by Albert Hyma, *The Christian Renaissance* (New York, 1925), pp. 309—326; his discussion of the differences between Luther and the so-called "Christian renaissance," pp. 326—329, betrays a grave misunderstanding of the meaning of the Reformation. For a sounder interpretation cf. Julius Hashagen, "Die 'devotio moderna'," *Zeitschrift fuer Kirchengeschichte,* LV (1936), pp. 523 ff.

[32] Paul Wernle, *Die Renaissance des Christentums im 16. Jahrhundert* (1904), suffers from the same oversimplification referred to above; on Erasmus, therefore, it is more satisfactory than on Luther. See Fritz Caspari, "Erasmus on the Social Functions of Christian Humanism," *Journal of the History of Ideas,* VIII (1947), pp. 78—106, for an analysis of the practical and political aspects of the *philosophia Christi.*

[33] Walther Koehler, *Wie Luther den Deutschen das Leben Jesu erzaehlt hat*, No. 127—128 of "Schriften des Vereins fuer Reformationsgeschichte" (Leipzig, 1917), for selections from Luther bearing this out.

[34] "De Servo Arbitrio," *WA* XVIII, 600—787. See the discussion of R. Hermann, *Zu Luthers Lehre vom unfreien Willen*, Vol. IV of "Greifswalder Studien zur Lutherforschung und neuzeitlichen Geistesgeschichte" (Greifswald, 1931). There is a useful outline of "De Servo Arbitrio" in *Lehre und Wehre*, XXIV (1878), pp. 321—335.

[35] It was a Christmas sermon delivered on December 25, 1514, *WA* I, 20—29.

[36] *WA* I, 355 ff.

[37] *WA* I, 226.

[38] "An christlichen Adel deutscher Nation," *WA* V, 457—458; cf. Luther to Spalatin, March 13, 1519, *WA Briefe*, I, 359.

[39] E. G. Sihler, "Luther and the Classics," in W. H. T. Dau (ed.), *Four Hundred Years* (St. Louis, 1916), pp. 240—254.

[40] As early as 1509 he was suspicious of Aristotle's influence in the Church: "Randbemerkungen zu De civitate Dei," *WA* IX, 27.

[41] On Thomas' reference to "that philosopher" cf., among others, the recent introduction by Anton C. Pegis to the Modern Library's *Introduction to Saint Thomas Acquinas* (New York, 1948), pp. xxvii—xxx; for Luther cf. "An christlichen Adel," *WA* VI, 457.

[42] Cf. Friedrich Nitzsch, *Luther und Aristoteles* (Kiel, 1883), p. 3 ff.: "Erzverleumder, Komoediant und Teufel . . . dreikoepfiger Cerberus . . . heidnische Bestie, der blinde heidnische Meister, der verdammte, hochmuetige schalkhafte Heide . . ."

[43] "An christlichen Adel," *WA* VI, 458; cf. also *WA Ti*, I, 57—58.

[44] Cf. Ch. II, note 27, below.

[45] Nels F. S. Ferré, *Reason and the Christian Faith*, I, *Faith and Reason* (New York, 1946), p. 142.

[46] "Der glaub fordert nit kundtschaft, wissenhait oder sicherheit, Sonnder frey ergeben und froelich wagen auff sein unempfundene, unversuchte, unerkannte guete," *WA* X—3, 239. See the excellent summary of Luther's understanding of faith by Wilhelm Pauck, "Luther's Faith" in his book *The Heritage of the Reformation* (Boston, 1950), pp. 15—23.

[47] Franz Pieper, *Christliche Dogmatik*, II (St. Louis, 1917), pp. 627—628.

[48] W. Link, *Das Ringen Luthers um die Freiheit der Theologie von der Philosophie* (Muenchen, 1940), to my knowledge the most satisfactory discussion of the entire problem. My study owes much to Link's analysis.

49 Luther's statement on Aristotle in "An christlichen Adel," referred to in note 38 above, endorses Aristotle's logical writings.

50 "Vom Abendmahl Christi. Bekenntnis," *WA* XXVI, 339; *WA* XXVI, 383—384, and *passim* throughout the treatise.

51 See, for example, *WA Ti* V, 556—567, for some examples of Luther's favorable statements on dialectics; in general see the index under "Dialectica."

52 On the activity of Luther's editors and compilers, cf. Preserved Smith, *Luther's Table Talk, A Critical Study* (New York, 1907), pp. 15—37; on their reliability, *ibid.,* pp. 99—110.

53 The so-called "Luther's Dialektik," dated by Walch around 1540, appears in *Dr. Martin Luthers Saemmtliche Schriften* (St. Louis, 1880 ff.; henceforth abbreviated as *StL*), XIV, 742—763; it is a dialectical compend that may well have come out of Melanchthon's classroom, but not out of Luther's.

54 This was Erasmus' charge, "De libero arbitrio diatribe," *StL* XVIII, 1611.

55 The latest to deal with the problem is Emil Brunner, *Man in Revolt. A Christian Anthropology,* translated by Olive Wyon (Philadelphia, 1947), pp. 267—273.

56 "De Servo Arbitrio," *WA* XVIII, 617—618 on Vergil.

57 Cf., for example, "De divinitate et humanitate Christi" (1540), *WA* XXXIX—2, 111; see the index to the disputations *sub voce* "Philosophie."

58 On disputations cf. the comments of Paul Drews, "Bemerkungen zu den akademischen Disputationen Melanchthons," *Theologische Studien und Kritiken,* LXIX (1896), p. 325 ff.

59 See Karl Holl, "Die Rechtfertigungslehre in Luthers Vorlesung ueber den Roemerbrief," *Luther,* p. 117, note 2.

60 There are probably several factors involved in addition to those mentioned in the text: Luther's resentment of the scholastics; his devotion to Biblical exegesis; his Augustinianism, which frequently produces an aversion to systematic presentation. Above all, Luther's existential approach prevented him from the sort of "system" that characterized both Roman Catholic and Protestant scholasticism.

61 See the references in Karl Holl, "Luthers Urteile ueber sich selbst," *Luther,* esp. pp. 398—401.

62 *Concordia Triglotta,* edited by F. Bente and W. H. T. Dau (St. Louis, 1921), pp. 461—463, for the systematic presentation, followed by a discussion of the Roman mass, p. 463 ff.

63 "Vom Abendmahl Christi. Bekenntnis," *WA* XXVI, 499.

[64] W. Gasz, *Geschichte der protestantischen Dogmatik*, I (Berlin, 1854), pp. 21—50, analyzes the differences between Luther and Melanchthon which made the latter the systematizer of the Reformation.

[65] Aristotle, *Protreptikos*, quoted in Jacques Maritain, *An Introduction to Philosophy*, translated by E. I. Watkin (New York, n. d.), p. 104. Cf. Clement of Alexandria, *Stromata*, Book VI, Ch. XVIII.

[66] Cf. Daniel Day Williams, "Brunner and Barth on Philosophy," *The Journal of Religion*, XXVII (1947), pp. 241—254.

[67] On this problem, see the discussions in Chapters II and III of this study.

[68] For a curious presentation of a species of existentialism, see Jacques Maritain, *Existence and the Existent* (New York, 1948). The best brief historical discussion of existentialism known to me is the essay by an outstanding representative of an existentially oriented philosophical theology: Paul Tillich, "Existential Philosophy," *Journal of the History of Ideas*, V (1944), pp. 44—70.

[69] See also our discussion of the relation between Kierkegaard and Luther in Ch. V, notes 101—117.

[70] Ferré, *op. cit.*, pp. 4—10, esp. pp. 6—8.

[71] See the unusual approach of Erdmann Schott, "Luthers Anthropologie und seine Lehre von der manducatio oralis in wechselseitiger Beleuchtung," *Zeitschrift fuer systematische Theologie*, IX (1931—1932), pp. 585—602.

[72] Wilhelm Braun, *Die Bedeutung der Concupiscenz in Luthers Leben und Lehre* (Berlin, 1908).

[73] See the several passages on flesh and spirit quoted by Holl, "Was verstand Luther unter Religion?", *Luther*, p. 62, notes 1—2.

[74] The discussion of Julius Mueller, *Die christliche Lehre von der Suende*, I (revised edition; Breslau, 1844), pp. 350—402, though in many ways outdated, is still relevant and useful.

[75] Cf., for example, *WA* II, 585—587.

[76] Luther's most detailed commentary on 1 Corinthians 15 appears *WA* XXXVI, 478—696; it would deserve translation.

[77] On flesh and spirit cf. Edgar Carlson's summary of Swedish Luther-research, *The Reinterpretation of Luther* (Philadelphia, 1948), pp. 51—57.

[78] Jaroslav Pelikan, "The Origins of the Object-Subject Antithesis in Lutheran Dogmatics," *Concordia Theological Monthly*, XXI (1950), pp. 94—104.

[79] Emil Brunner, *The Divine-Human Encounter* (Philadelphia, 1943).

[80] Gustaf Aulén, *The Faith of the Christian Church*, translated by Eric H. Wahlstrom and G. Everett Arden (Philadelphia, 1948), p. 16.

[81] See Ch. V, notes 99—100, below.

[82] See the bibliography cited in M. Reu, *Luther and the Scriptures* (Columbus, 1944).

[83] Cf. Franz Pieper, *Christliche Dogmatik*, I (St. Louis, 1924), pp. 334—360; on the primacy of Christ, see esp. pp. 353—356.

[84] On Luther's Christocentric approach to the Scripture, see the excellent articles of F. A. Hoppe, "Grundzuege der lutherischen Hermeneutik zusammengestellt aus Luther's Schriften," *Lehre und Wehre*, XXVIII (1882), 57—72, 108—111, 148—157.

[85] "Deudsch Catechismus," *WA* XXX—1, 132—133 is the most familiar, but by no means the only place this occurs; on the background of the phrase in Augustine and the mystics, cf. Karl Holl, "Was verstand Luther unter Religion?" *Luther*, p. 84, note 4.

[86] See Karl Holl, "Der Neubau der Sittlichkeit," *Luther*, pp. 247—250.

[87] "Ein Unterrichtung wie sich die Christen ynn Mosen sollen schicken," *WA* XXIV, 12—13. The entire treatise is revelatory of Luther's existential understanding of the Word of God.

[88] On Luther's view of the Word, cf. Carlson, *op. cit.*, pp. 117—127.

[89] Sermon on St. Matt. 21:1-9, *StL* XI, 28—29.

[90] Werner Elert, *Morphologie des Luthertums* (2 vols.; Muenchen, 1931 to 1932), I, p. 60, pp. 165—166.

[91] So, to cite but one instance, in "Ad librum . . . Catharini . . . responsio" (1521): "non de Euangelio scripto sed vocali loquor," *WA* VII, 721.

[92] Karl Holl, "Die Rechtfertigungslehre in Luthers Vorlesung ueber den Roemerbrief," *Luther*, p. 118, note 2.

[93] Many "Lutheran" answers to Brunner's theology have unfortunately been informed more by Fundamentalist than by Lutheran theology. Brunner is certainly not free of involvement in the very subjectivism he repudiates.

[94] Marjorie Grene, *Dreadful Freedom* (Chicago, 1948), is a telling analysis of existential pessimism.

[95] Cf. Ch. V, notes 113—114, below.

[96] Rudolf Otto, *The Idea of the Holy*, translated by John W. Harvey (London, 1946), pp. 8—41.

[97] Jean-Paul Sartre, *Existentialism* (New York, 1948), is a clear exposition of atheistic, humanistic existentialism.

[98] On the *Anfechtungen*, cf. Heinrich Boehmer, *Road to Reformation*, pp. 87—111, and the stirring exposition of Roland Bainton, "Luther's Struggle for Faith," *Church History*, XVII (1948), pp. 193—206.

[99] "Resolutiones disputationum de indulgentiarum virtute," *WA* I, 557.

[100] "Enarratio Psalmi XC," *WA* XL—3, 534—535. This discussion of death is classic and should certainly appear in English. For a brief exposition of Luther's *Angst* with other references, cf. my essay on "The Structure of Luther's Piety," pp. 13—16.

[101] Gustaf Aulén, *Christus Victor* (London, 1931).

[102] For a provocative interpretation of Luther's view of death, see Carl Stange, "Luthers Gedanken ueber Tod, Gericht und ewiges Leben," *Zeitschrift fuer systematische Theologie,* X (1933), pp. 490—513.

[103] Sören Kierkegaard, *Concluding Unscientific Postscript to the "Philosophical Fragments,"* translated by David F. Swenson and Walter Lowrie (Princeton, 1941), p. 386; on *Angst,* cf. Kierkegaard's moving *The Concept of Dread,* translated by Walter Lowrie (Princeton, 1944).

[104] Werner Elert, "Angst und Einsamkeit in der Geschichte des Luthertums," *Jahrbuch fuer die evangelisch-lutherische Landeskirche Bayerns* (1925 to 1926), p. 6 ff.

[105] See the celebrated "five ways" of Thomas Aquinas, *Summa Theologica,* Question 2, Article 3, in Anton C. Pegis (ed.), *Basic Writings of Saint Thomas Aquinas* (2 vols.; New York, 1945), I, pp. 22—23.

[106] Karl Barth, *The Epistle to the Romans,* translated by Edwyn C. Hoskyns (London, 1933), pp. 45—48.

[107] Martin Luther, *Vorlesung ueber den Roemerbrief 1515—1516,* translated by Eduard Ellwein (2nd ed.; Muenchen, 1928), pp. 24—31.

[108] Karl August Meissinger, *Luthers Exegese in der Fruehzeit* (Leipzig, 1911).

[109] Cf. Boehmer, *op. cit.,* pp. 88—89.

[110] Ernst Schaefer, *Luther als Kirchenhistoriker* (Guetersloh, 1897).

[111] This did not characterize later Lutherans; cf. Ch. II, notes 60—61, and Ch. III, notes 98—111, below.

[112] Cf. Philip S. Watson, *Let God Be God! An Interpretation of the Theology of Martin Luther* (Philadelphia, 1948), p. 84.

[113] For example, *WA* XLII, 291—292.

[114] Watson's discussion of natural theology in Luther, *loc. cit.,* bears out this Thomistic distinction.

[115] Cf. Ch. II, note 61, below.

[116] *Revelation and Reason,* p. 70, note 13.

[117] The most authoritative study of the differences between Luther and the Enthusiasts is Karl Holl, "Luther und die Schwaermer," *Luther,* pp. 420—467.

[118] "Ein Unterrichtung," *WA* XXIV, 10.

[119] Edgar Carlson has summarized Luther's theology of government in his essay "Luther's Conception of Government," *Church History,* XV (1946), pp. 257—270.

[120] Ernst Troeltsch, *Die Soziallehren der christlichen Kirchen und Gruppen* (Tuebingen, 1923), p. 494 ff. But see the sharp critique of Troeltsch in Holl's essay "Der Neubau der Sittlichkeit," *Luther,* pp. 155—287; on the Sermon on the Mount, see his discussion of Troeltsch, pp. 248—249, note 4.

NOTES TO CHAPTER II

[1] In addition to the interpretations of Hildebrandt, Engelland, Caemmerer, and others referred to in the notes below, see the essay of Reinhold Seeberg "Melanchthons Stellung in der Geschichte des Dogmas und der Dogmatik," *Neue kirchliche Zeitschrift,* VII (1897), p. 126 ff.; also C. E. J. Ratz, "Was hat Luther durch Melanchthon gewonnen?", *Zeitschrift fuer historische Theologie,* XL (1870), pp. 313—386.

[2] *WA Ti,* III, 460.

[3] See Luther's famous words of 1529: "Ich bin dazu geboren, das ich mit den rotten und teuffeln mus kriegen und zu felde ligen, darumb meiner buecher viel stuermisch und kriegisch sind. . . . Aber M. Philipps feret seuberlich und still daher, bawet und pflantzet, sehet und begeust mit lust, nach dem Gott yhm hat gegeben seine gaben reichlich," "Vorrede zu Melanchthons Auslegung des Kolosserbriefs," *WA* XXX—2, 68—69.

[4] Luther to Justus Jonas, July 21, 1530, *StL* XVI, 2323. See other passages cited in F. Bente's Introduction to *Concordia Triglotta,* pp. 19—20. The entire question of Luther's attitude toward the Augustana, important here as an indication of his attitude toward Melanchthon, is put in a new light by the researches of M. Reu, *The Augsburg Confession* (Chicago, 1930), I, pp. 54—113, esp. pp. 69—75.

[5] Thus, for example, during the negotiations connected with the Wittenberg Concord of 1536; cf. my essay "Luther's Endorsement of the *Confessio Bohemica,*" *Concordia Theological Monthly,* XX (1949), p. 839, note 56.

[6] *WA Ti* V, 205.

[7] *WA Ti* V, 435.

[8] "De Servo Arbitrio," *WA* XVIII, 601.

[9] Cf. Karl Holl, "Luthers Urteile ueber sich selbst," *Luther,* pp. 398—401.

10 Cf., for one example, "Enarrationes epistolarum et evangeliorum, quas postillas vocant," *WA* VII, 463; there are several similar statements in Luther's letters.

11 See the passages cited in Franz Hildebrandt, *Melanchthon: Alien or Ally?* (Cambridge, 1946), "Prelude," pp. xviii—xix.

12 Bente, *op. cit.,* pp. 102—195.

13 W. Gasz, *Calixt und der Syncretismus* (Breslau, 1846), has evaluated the continuing influence of Melanchthonianism at the University of Helmstaedt and its influence on Calixtus.

14 "Die Rechtfertigungslehre in Luthers Vorlesung ueber den Roemerbrief mit besonderer Ruecksicht auf die Frage der Heilsgewiszheit," *Luther,* pp. 126—129.

15 For an important phase of this research, see the recent book by Edgar M. Carlson, *The Reinterpretation of Luther* (Philadelphia, 1948).

16 R. R. Caemmerer, "The Melanchthonian Blight," *Concordia Theological Monthly,* XVIII (1947), pp. 321—338.

17 *CR* XIII, 5—178.

18 Erasmus' *De libero arbitrio Diatribe* was edited by Johann von Walter in 1910; for the sake of convenience I have used the translation in *StL* XVIII, 1600—1669; Luther's *De servo arbitrio* appears *WA* XVIII, 600—787, on which see also Ch. I, note 34, above.

19 "Nam perinde ut tyrannus est in republica, ita voluntas in homine," quoted in Peter Petersen, *Geschichte der aristotelischen Philosophie im protestantischen Deutschland* (Leipzig, 1921), p. 100; cf. also *CR* XXI, 14.

20 Cf. *CR* XIII, 16 on the rational, immortal soul as the distinctive part of man.

21 Friedrich Paulsen, *Geschichte des gelehrten Unterrichts* (2nd ed.; Leipzig, 1896), I, p. 437 ff.

22 Hans Engelland, *Melanchthon. Glauben und Handeln* (Muenchen, 1931), p. 225 ff., on the necessity of religious certainty. Of all the interpretations of Melanchthon known to me, Engelland's is outstanding, in spite of his Barthian propensities.

23 On *certitudo* in Melanchthon, cf. Caemmerer, *op. cit.,* pp. 328—329.

24 See especially the passages from *De anima* referred to in notes 58—59 of this chapter.

25 Reuchlin was instrumental in bringing Melanchthon to Wittenberg; see his letter to Melanchthon, July 24, 1518, *CR* I, 32.

[26] Cf. Melanchthon to Spalatin, March 13, 1519, *CR* I, 75, on his desire to edit some of Aristotle.

[27] *CR* IX, 700.

[28] On the circumstances attending Melanchthon's appointment cf. Karl Sell, *Philipp Melanchthon und die deutsche Reformation bis 1531,* No. 56 of "Schriften des Vereins fuer Reformationsgeschichte" (Halle, 1897), pp. 10—14.

[29] *CR* I, 269; I, 96.

[30] From what followed (see also notes 40—41 below), it seems doubtful that Melanchthon ever made a clear break. He seems rather to have sought the same ends in theology which had attracted him to humanistic scholarship.

[31] Melanchthon to Johann Lang, April 1520, *CR* I, 163.

[32] See his treatise on the study of Pauline theology, *CR* XI, 36.

[33] Cf. Melanchthon to Johann Hess, April 17, 1520, *CR* I, 158—159, on the background of the *Loci.*

[34] Volume XXI of the *Corpus Reformatorum* presents the evolution of the *Loci* from the simple form of 1521 to the later compends.

[35] On Melanchthon's relations with Erasmus, see his statements in a letter to the great humanist, *CR* III, 68—69.

[36] See our discussion in Ch. I, notes 31—34, above.

[37] On the influence of classical rhetoric upon Protestant hermeneutics, see the comments of Wilhelm Dilthey, *Gesammelte Schriften,* II (Leipzig, 1914), pp. 118—122. There is need for a thorough investigation of this problem, since only one part of it — the work of Flacius — has been covered by Guenther Moldaenke, *Schriftverstaendnis und Schriftdeutung im Zeitalter der Reformation,* I, *Matthias Flacius Illyricus* (Stuttgart, 1936).

[38] Karl Holl, "Luthers Bedeutung fuer den Fortschritt der Auslegungskunst," *Luther,* pp. 544—582; cf. the brief chapter on "The Bible and the Reformation" in Robert M. Grant, *The Bible in the Church* (New York, 1948), pp. 109—117.

[39] For humanist methodology, see the analysis of Richard P. McKeon, "Renaissance and Method," *Studies in the History of Ideas,* III (New York, 1935), p. 71 ff.

[40] *CR* I, 607.

[41] Petersen, *op. cit.,* pp. 29—30, presents a psychological analysis to demonstrate that Melanchthon never broke with Aristotelianism, even in the years 1518 to 1521; but see statements like those in his letter to Bartholomew Schaller, February 1, 1520, *CR* I, 132.

[42] See *CR* XI, 653; XIII, 381, and other passages.

[43] *WA Ti* XIV, 14.

[44] On Cicero's philosophical significance, see Charles Norris Cochrane, *Christianity and Classical Culture,* pp. 38—43; on Melanchthon's attitude toward Cicero, for instance, *CR* II, 543.

[45] *CR* I, 74.

[46] On the purpose of the *Loci* and their relation to the *Summae,* see the introduction to Theodor Kolde (ed.), *Loci Communes Philipp Melanchthons in ihrer Urgestalt nach Plitt* (4th ed.; Erlangen, 1925).

[47] Paul Joachimsen, "Loci communes. Eine Untersuchung zur Geistes-geschichte des Humanismus und der Reformation," *Luther, Jahrbuch der Luther-Gesellschaft* (Muenchen, 1926).

[48] On the history of the *Loci* and their publication, see Charles Leander Hill, "Introduction" to his translation of the *Loci* (Boston, 1944), pp. 50—62; Hill's "critical estimate," pp. 29—49 is directed by a curious interpretation of both Luther and Melanchthon and by a consequent failure to fix Melanchthon's place between Luther and later Lutheranism.

[49] In fact, it was the preface to this edition which produced the magnificently evangelical and existential statement "Hoc est Christum cognoscere, beneficia eius cognoscere," marking a clear break with all speculation.

[50] Th. Heppe sees the first edition of the *Loci* as providing a point of departure for the later aberrations, "Die Ansaetze der spaeteren theologischen Entwicklung Melanchthons in den Loci von 1521," *Zeitschrift fuer systematische Theologie,* VI (1928), 599—615.

[51] For Melanchthon's interpretation of Aristotelian causality, see his extended discussion, *CR* XIII, 673—685.

[52] On Melanchthon's work in the field of logic, cf. Petersen, *op. cit.,* p. 64 ff.

[53] "Declamatio de philosophia," *CR* XI.

[54] *CR* XI, 281.

[55] On the relation of philosophy and Gospel, see his remarks, *CR* XII, 689—690; see also the many passages quoted in Hildebrandt, *op. cit.,* pp. 18—26.

[56] See notes 19 ff. of this chapter.

[57] Cf. his "Oratio de dialectica," *CR* XI, 159—163.

[58] "De anima," *CR* XIII, 150—151.

[59] *CR* XIII, 151.

[60] Ernst Troeltsch, *Vernunft und Offenbarung bei Johann Gerhard und Melanchthon. Untersuchung zur Geschichte der altprotestantischen Theologie* (Goettingen, 1891) is a careful and provocative study of natural theology in the first century of Lutheranism; see Ch. III, notes 98 ff., below.

[61] *CR* XIII, 198: God is, among other things, "sapiens, *beneficus, justus* . . ."

[62] *CR* XIII, 222 ff. On this problem in later Orthodoxy, see Ch. III, notes 112—113, below.

[63] *CR* XXI, 370; X, 690.

[64] His inaugural address at Wittenberg, August 29, 1518, was entitled "De corrigendis adolescentium studiis," *CR* XI, 15—25.

[65] *CR* XI, 280; I, 613.

[66] Caemmerer, *op. cit.,* p. 336, with full references.

[67] *Ibid.*

[68] *CR* XI, 501; cf. Ch. I, note 38, above.

[69] On Melanchthon's scientific interests, with special reference to astrology, cf. Lynn Thorndike, *A History of Magic and Experimental Science,* V (New York, 1941), pp. 378—405.

[70] See Ch. III, notes 3—12, below.

[71] Ch. I, note 118, above.

[72] This development is traced in any standard history of the Reformation; Preserved Smith, *Age of the Reformation,* esp. pp. 116—135, is a handy though somewhat unbalanced account.

[73] Karl Holl, "Luther und das landesherrliche Kirchenregiment," *Luther,* pp. 326—380.

[74] Cf. the statement of the Wittenberg faculty in 1638, quoted in Karl Hase (ed.), *Hutterus Redivivus* (Leipzig, 1829), p. 353.

[75] Karl Holl, "Luther und die Schwaermer," *Luther,* pp. 420—467.

[76] The very existence of the Reformation, politically speaking, depended upon its alliance with the German princes; hence it opposed Roman Catholic pretensions on both religious and political grounds.

[77] Ch. I, note 117, above.

[78] On the entire problem, see Richard Nuernberger, *Kirche und weltliche Obrigkeit bei Melanchthon* (Wuerzburg, 1937).

[79] For a summary of Aristotle's political philosophy, including the contrast with Plato, see William Archibald Dunning, *A History of Political Theories,* I, *Ancient and Medieval* (New York, 1908), pp. 49—98.

[80] *The Basic Works of Aristotle,* edited by Richard P. McKeon (New York, 1944), pp. 1127—1316; on revolutions, esp. pp. 1232—1264.

[81] Otto Piper, "The Political Structure of Lutheranism," mimeographed essay delivered at the Social Ethics seminar of Valparaiso University, p. 33.

[82] Cf. Werner Elert, "Zur Terminologie der Staatslehre Melanchthons und seiner Schueler," *Zeitschrift fuer systematische Theologie,* IX (1931—1932), pp. 522—534.

[83] *Concordia Triglotta,* p. 123.

[84] On Melanchthon's ethics, see Herrlinger's *Die Theologie Melanchthons in ihrer geschichtlichen Entwicklung* (Gotha, 1879), pp. 209—343.

[85] There is perhaps no more pressing need in present American Lutheran theological scholarship than a detailed commentary on the Lutheran Confessions. I have pointed to their uniqueness in my essay "The Relation of Faith and Knowledge in the Lutheran Confessions," *Concordia Theological Monthly,* XXI (1950), pp. 321—331.

[86] See the comments of Carlson, *op. cit.,* pp. 36—44, on the "historical-systematic" method of the Lundensian theologians; on "Konfessionskunde," cf. J. L. Neve, *Churches and Sects of Christendom* (revised edition; Blair, 1944), pp. 35—38.

[87] Bente, *op. cit.,* pp. 144—152; Fr. H. R. Frank, *Die Theologie der Konkordienformel historisch-dogmatisch entwickelt und beleuchtet* (Erlangen, 1858 ff.), I, 50—240; and Wilhelm Preger, *Matthias Flacius Illyricus und seine Zeit* (2 vols.; Erlangen, 1859—1860), II, pp. 310—412 and *passim.*

[88] Cf. the discussion of Frank, *op. cit.,* I, p. 67 ff.

[89] *Ibid.,* pp. 96—97, notes 59—62.

[90] Preger, *op. cit.,* II, 395—412; Preger's presentation is unfortunately influenced by his evident animus in favor of Flacius and his desire to defend his hero against calumnies past and present.

[91] Melanchthon's most complete discussion of *substantia* appears in *CR* XIII, 528 ff.; Aristotle's own distinction of substance and accident is developed in his *Metaphysics,* Book V, Ch. 30, *Basic Works,* p. 777.

[92] Petersen has carefully evaluated Melanchthon's use of Aristotle in the problem of substance, *op. cit.,* pp. 69—71.

[93] *CR* XIII, 523.

[94] Frank, *op. cit.,* I, pp. 68—69.

[95] Preger, *op. cit.,* II, pp. 398—405.

[96] *Ibid.,* p. 399, note 3.

97 See Flacius' own brief statement of the relation between philosophy and theology *sub voce* "Philosophia," *Clavis Scripturae Sacrae* (Jena, 1674), I, p. 914.

98 Quoted in Bente, *op. cit.,* p. 136.

99 On Flacius' doctrine of man and the final outcome of the controversy, cf. my essay "The Doctrine of Man in the Lutheran Confessions," *The Lutheran Quarterly,* II (1950), pp. 34—44, with detailed reference to sixteenth-century theologians.

100 Emil Brunner, *Revelation and Reason,* pp. 77—80 for the latest stage of their discussion on revelation in the creation.

101 1 John 4:8. This passage, which is usually ignored in discussions of the natural knowledge of God, is significant also because only a Christian is capable of the *agape* which is here stated as necessary for the knowledge of God.

102 On Flacius and Barth, see my "Doctrine of Man," p. 41, note 32.

103 Preger, *op. cit.,* II, pp. 212—214.

104 The standard interpretation of Osiander is that of W. Moeller, *Andreas Osiander, Leben und ausgewaehlte Schriften* (Elberfeld, 1870). It has in many respects been replaced by Emmanuel Hirsch, *Die Theologie des Andreas Osiander und ihre geschichtlichen Voraussetzungen* (Goettingen, 1919).

105 Cf. Fr. Frank, *op. cit.,* II, pp. 1—147, for a careful study of the Osiandrian controversy as it relates to the Formula of Concord. See also the interpretation of Gustaf Aulén, *Christus Victor,* p. 139 ff.

106 Cf. Albrecht Ritschl, "Die Rechtfertigungslehre des Andreas Osiander," *Jahrbuecher fuer deutsche Theologie,* II (1857), p. 795 ff. Ritschl's views were revised by his son, Otto Ritschl, *Dogmengeschichte des Protestantismus* (Leipzig, 1908 ff.), II—1, p. 455 ff.

107 So, for example, his speculation on whether Christ would have become incarnate even without the intervention of human sin.

108 Karl Holl, "Die Rechtfertigungslehre in Luthers Vorlesung ueber den Roemerbrief," *Luther,* pp. 126—129; in this context I do not wish to involve myself in a discussion of the controversy between Holl and Wilhelm Walther of Rostock on Luther's doctrine of justification. My own interpretation of the problem is substantially that of T. A. Kantonen, *Resurgence of the Gospel* (Philadelphia, 1948), pp. 50—51, with perhaps the added comment that as Holl misunderstood Luther, so Wilhelm Walther misunderstood Melanchthon.

109 On Melanchthon's opposition to Osiander, see Moeller, *op. cit.,* pp. 478 to 491.

110 For an evaluation of Melanchthon's doctrine of justification and of its ethical implications, cf. Hirsch, *op. cit.,* p. 229 ff.

111 Caemmerer, *op. cit.,* p. 336, note 46.

112 Adolf Koeberle, *The Quest for Holiness,* translated by John C. Mattes (New York, 1936); see also the neglected essay of Ed. Preuss, *Die Rechtfertigung des Suenders vor Gott* (2nd ed.; Berlin, 1871), in which the best that the dogmaticians of the seventeenth century had to say about justification is brought together.

113 Otto Ritschl's discussion, referred to in note 106 above, makes the affinities between Osiander's view and the Roman position clear.

114 The degree to which Melanchthon's intellectualism is perceptible even in those who opposed his theological formulations would be a worth-while subject for investigation; I have attempted to evaluate this factor in this second chapter, but more detailed research would be necessary before final conclusions could be drawn.

115 C. F. W. Walther, *Der Concordienformel Kern und Stern* (2nd ed.; St. Louis, 1877), I, p. 60.

116 While a student at Wittenberg, Chemnitz became so enamored of astrology (cf. note 69 of this chapter) that he missed some of Luther's lectures to devote his time to astrological study.

117 Bente, *op. cit.,* pp. 245—247.

118 F. E. Mayer, "Ist die Variata synergistisch und majoristisch?" *Concordia Theological Monthly,* VI (1935), pp. 254—267, on Melanchthon's humanistic synergism and his unionism.

119 *CR* XXI, 658—663.

120 Fr. Frank, *op. cit.,* I, pp. 130—137.

121 *Concordia Triglotta,* pp. 785—791; pp. 881—915.

122 Charles P. Krauth, *The Conservative Reformation and Its Theology* (Philadelphia, 1913), pp. 326—328.

123 G. Kawerau, *Die Versuche, Melanchthon zur katholischen Kirche zurueckzufuehren,* No. 73 of "Schriften des Vereins fuer Reformationsgeschichte" (Halle, 1902), esp. p. 73 ff. on Trent.

124 Cf. Melanchthon's letter to Calvin, October 14, 1554, *CR* VIII, 362.

125 *Concordia Triglotta,* pp. 807—827; pp. 971—1049.

126 *De duabus naturis in Christo, de hypostatica earum unione* (Leipzig, 1600). See the brief evaluation of Chemnitz' Christology by J. A. Dorner, *History of the Development of the Doctrine of the Person of Christ,* translated by D. W. Simon, Division Second, II (Edinburgh, 1882), pp. 198—208.

[127] The late Dr. Krauth's *Conservative Reformation,* referred to in note 122 above, is the outstanding English exposition of this thesis; it should be revised, as mentioned in note 85 above, and combined with a study of the Formula on the basis of the best available literature.

[128] Interestingly, historians of the Formula, like Frank and Krauth, have restricted themselves to its theological importance; Chemnitz' role in rescuing Melanchthonian philosophy has been neglected.

[129] *Loci theologici reuerendi et clarissimi viri, D. Martini Chemnitii,* edited by Polycarp Leyser (Franckfort, 1591).

[130] Cf. Franz Pieper, *Christliche Dogmatik,* II, p. 174, note 575; Dr. Pieper does not refer to the fact that several sections of the 1591 edition of Chemnitz' *Loci* were not inserted by Chemnitz, but by Leyser: so in the doctrines of original sin, where he inserts an older treatise of Chemnitz against the Flacians, and of good works, where a similar section occurs.

[131] The title contains the phrase: ". . . quibus et loci communes D. Philippi Melanchthonis perspicue explicantur et quasi integrum christianae doctrinae corpus ecclesiae dei syncere proponitur."

[132] Cf. Ch. III, note 82, below.

[133] W. Gasz, *Geschichte der protestantischen Dogmatik,* I, pp. 70—76, has suggested Chemnitz' crucial position in the transitional generation between the Reformation and Orthodoxy, but his sketchy discussion should be more fully presented, since it strikes at a central problem of Lutheran theological history: How did Luther's Reformation produce later Lutheran theology?

[134] Cf. Johann Salomon Semler, "Einleitung in die dogmatische Gottes-gelehrsamkeit," preface to Siegmund Jacob Baumgarten, *Evangelische Glaubens-lehre,* II (Halle, 1760), p. 150 ff., for an enumeration of the dogmatic works that can be traced to Melanchthon's influence.

[135] On the use of the philosophical terms *substantia* and *accidens* in the Formula of Concord, see the penetrating comments of Edmund Schlink, *Theologie der lutherischen Bekenntnisschriften* (2nd ed.; Munich, 1946), pp. 78—79, footnote 11. Schlink's work is almost indispensable for the study of any problem in the theology of the Lutheran Confessions.

[136] *Concordia Triglotta,* p. 877.

[137] Most readily available in Karl Hase's recension, *Hutterus Redivivus oder Dogmatik der evangelisch-lutherischen Kirche* (Leipzig, 1829).

[138] Hutter quotes Melanchthon only "ubi quidem ille orthodoxian tenuit," quoted in Gasz, *Geschichte,* I, p. 253.

[139] Gasz' evaluation of Hutter, *ibid.,* pp. 251—259, is somewhat overdrawn, but its central thesis — that Hutter represents the next stage after Chemnitz — is probably quite accurate.

NOTES TO CHAPTER III

[1] There is, at any rate, no known instance in the history of Christian thought when such a "system" was produced without the aid of philosophy; see, in general, the concluding comments of this study.

[2] The late Veit Valentin laments the cultural decline in Germany after the Reformation: *The German People,* translated by Olga Marx (New York, 1946), pp. 174—175. His discussion of the Reformation, which otherwise provides many brilliant insights, fails to deal with the education impact of the work of Luther and Melanchthon; cf. notes 16—17 below.

[3] On the curricular reorganization of the secondary and elementary schools, cf. Ferdinand Cohrs, *Philipp Melanchthon Deutschlands Lehrer,* No. 55 of "Schriften des Vereins fuer Reformationsgeschichte" (Halle, 1897), pp. 49—58, esp. the sample lesson plan, p. 55.

[4] Heinrich Boehmer, *Road to Reformation,* pp. 7—10.

[5] Calvin, Erasmus, Melanchthon all took part in the publication of various classical texts.

[6] Cf. Cohrs, *op. cit.,* pp. 31—48.

[7] On the place of dialectics, *ibid.,* p. 57.

[8] Cf. Werner Elert, *Morphologie des Luthertums,* II, pp. 350—366: "Im Strom der Rechtsgeschichte."

[9] See Ch. II, note 82 above.

[10] In addition, of course, to the works of Galen and Hippocrates, which were required in medical study.

[11] Cf. Carl Schmidt, *Philipp Melanchthon* (Eberfeld, 1861), pp. 676—692 on the work of Melanchthon and his associates in this regard.

[12] Cf. *CR* XIII, 507—510, for an enumeration of the editions of Melanchthon's handbooks.

[13] Emil Weber, *Die philosophische Scholastik des deutschen Protestantismus im Zeitalter der Orthodoxie* (Leipzig, 1907), pp. 14—15.

[14] On the continued reverence for Melanchthon, see the long footnote in Peter Petersen, *Geschichte der aristotelischen Philosophie im protestantischen Deutschland,* pp. 125—126.

[15] Weber, *loc. cit.*

[16] See Petersen's detailed account, *op. cit.,* pp. 109—218, of the expansion and establishment of Aristotelian philosophy.

[17] Weber, *op. cit.,* pp. 27—34.

18 Entry into the learned professions and into government service was generally through university training. As this training became more and more Aristotelian, that philosophy gradually became the least common denominator of theologians, physicians, lawyers, and statesmen.

19 For one example of princely scholarship in theology, cf. August Tholuck, *Lebenszeugen der lutherischen Kirche aus allen Staenden vor und waehrend der Zeit des dreiszigjaehrigen Krieges* (Berlin, 1859), pp. 61—66.

20 Cf. G. Ellinger, "Neulateinische Dichtung Deutschlands im 16. Jahrhundert" in Paul Merker and Wolfgang Stammler (ed.), *Reallexikon der deutschen Literaturgeschichte,* II (Berlin, 1928), pp. 469—495.

21 Significantly, James Hastings Nichols' recent *Primer for Protestants* uses Trent as the dividing mark in Roman Catholic history.

22 *Examen Concilii Tridentini* (1565), edited by Ed. Preuss (Berlin, 1861). There is, unfortunately, no English translation or interpretation of the *Examen.* The German translation begun by C. A. Frank (St. Louis, 1875) was, to my knowledge, never completed.

23 See the careful analysis by Weber, *Philosophische Scholastik,* pp. 38-—45, including statistics on the frequency with which medieval scholastics are quoted in Orthodox works.

24 Cf., for example, *Examen,* p. 103, on the speculative and philosophical bent of Roman Catholic anthropology; *ibid.,* p. 379 on the Lord's Supper.

25 On this supposed coincidence of poor philosophy and poor theology, cf. the equation of the heathen and the Papists in the problem of certainty by Aegidius Hunnius, *Articulus de justificatione hominis* (Franckfort, 1590), p. 74.

26 Cf. the chapter "De doctrinae in Romana Ecclesia corruptione," *Confessio Catholica* (Jena, 1661), I, pp. 78—106, where the Roman Church is not criticized for corrupting its theology with philosophy. In his *Loci,* as in his disputations, Gerhard makes sympathetic use of Aquinas and other medieval philosophers; cf. *Loci Theologici,* edited by Ed. Preuss (Berlin, 1863 ff.), I, p. 520, on scholastic Christology.

27 See Johann Georg Walch, *Historische und Theologische Einleitung in die Religions-Streitigkeiten, welche sonderlich ausser der Evangelisch-Lutherischen Kirche entstanden* (Jena, 1733 ff.), III, pp. 780—852 for a listing of the chief Protestant works against Rome during the seventeenth century.

28 With the possible exception of Johann Gerhard, none of the dogmaticians even attempted to construct a Christian philosophy of culture; Gerhard was prevented by the press of controversy from completing the insights he had developed.

[29] It is significant that as early as 1583, Bonaventura's speculations about Christ were not criticized for their philosophical tone, but that actually the tone of the Lutheran answer is philosophical, too; cf. *Apologia oder Verantwortung des Christlichen Concordien-Buchs* (2nd ed.; Arnstadt, 1675), pp. 200—201. Even David Chytraeus, one of the authors of the Formula of Concord, refers favorably to scholastic speculation on the condition of the body in eternal life: *De morte et vita aeterna* (Wittenberg, 1591), pp. 244 to 245.

[30] Cf. the terse though one-sided discussion of the term and its implications by William Turner, "Scholasticism," *The Catholic Encyclopedia*, XIII, pp. 548 to 552.

[31] Franz Hildebrandt, *Melanchthon*, p. 2.

[32] Weber, *op. cit.*, p. 38 ff.

[33] Perhaps the best of these is Johann Gerhard, *Methodus studii theologiae* (Jena, 1620); on the scholastics, see p. 320. The libraries of Concordia Seminary and Valparaiso University have preserved many of these syllabi; an investigation of them would provide many insights into the Lutheran Church's life and thought in the seventeenth century.

[34] Balthasar Meisner, *Philosophia sobria* (3 vols.; Wittenberg, 1611—1625), II, p. 675. I have made use of Meisner's work in my essay on "The Object-Subject Antithesis," *Concordia Theological Monthly*, XXI (1950), pp. 101 to 103, notes 6, 21, 40.

[35] Cf. Abraham Calov, *Systema locorum theologicorum . . . doctrinam praxin et controversiarum fidei . . . pertractationem luculentam exhibens* (12 vols.; Wittenberg, 1655—1677), I, p. 76.

[36] Although there have been many works on this polemic since, the most detailed history of anti-Reformed polemics is Johann Georg Walch, *op. cit.* (see note 27 above), I, pp. 382—549 for a résumé, and all of Volume III for the complete exposition.

[37] Cf. Walch, *op. cit.*, III, pp. 155—158, for many references to this charge in the Lutheran literature of the seventeenth century.

[38] As Gustaf Aulén suggests, *The Faith of the Christian Church*, p. 57, the issue between "finitum capax infiniti" and "finitum non capax infiniti" is unfortunately phrased. The Biblical fact is "Infinitum capax finiti," or, perhaps better, "Infinitus"; and this is what Lutheranism meant to say. What was said often amounted to a defense of human capacity for the divine; this, like its Reformed antithesis, is bad philosophy and worse theology.

³⁹ Cf. Walch, *op. cit.,* III, pp. 238—239, p. 318, pp. 466—467 and 511—512 for a list of some of Calov's works against the Reformed; for some examples of Calov's dialectical subtlety, see his *Scripta philosophica* (Luebeck, 1651), *Metaphysica divina,* in which Aristotelian metaphysics appears as a divine science. For a somewhat slanted characterization of Calov, cf. August Tholuck, *Der Geist der lutherischen Theologen Wittenbergs im Verlauf des 17. Jahrhunderts* (Hamburg, 1852), pp. 185—211.

⁴⁰ Paul Althaus, *Die Prinzipienlehre der deutsch-reformierten Dogmatik im Zeitalter der aristotelischen Scholastik* (Leipzig, 1914), for a thorough and stimulating analysis.

⁴¹ The most complete Orthodox Reformed dogmatics I have at hand is Franciscus Turretinus, *Institutio Theologiae Elencticae* (3 vols.; Geneva, 1688 ff.); the discussion of law, for example, "Locus de Lege Dei," II, pp. 1—184, shows a carefulness of philosophical distinction combined with theological precision, especially in the considerations of natural law in relation to both divine and human positive law; see also the discussion of the relation of philosophy to theology, "Locus de Theologia," I, pp. 49—53.

⁴² John Neville Figgis, *Studies of Political Thought from Gerson to Grotius* (2nd ed.; Cambridge, 1931), pp. 167—191, esp. p. 185 ff.

⁴³ William Archibald Dunning, *A History of Political Theories,* II, *From Luther to Montesquieu,* pp. 153—191, is an excellent analysis of Grotius' thought in relation to his general world view and to the work of his predecessors.

⁴⁴ There is a brief discussion of this controversy in Franz Pieper, *Christliche Dogmatik,* II, pp. 337—358; see also the interesting though rather unbalanced account of J. A. Dorner, *History of the Development of the Doctrine of the Person of Christ,* Division Second, II, pp. 281—302.

⁴⁵ *Systema locorum theologicorum,* VII, p. 618.

⁴⁶ *Christliche Dogmatik,* II, pp. 345—358.

⁴⁷ This seems to have been almost inevitable in view of the problem considered: it is a question on which the New Testament is silent and which could not be answered except by recourse to metaphysical understandings of space and of matter foreign to the world of the New Testament.

⁴⁸ Calov's *Biblia Illustrata* is probably the outstanding exegetical work between the *Harmonia Evangelistarum,* a composite work in the last quarter of the sixteenth and first quarter of the seventeenth century, and Bengel's *Gnomon;* see also our comments in Ch. II, note 37, above.

⁴⁹ See the remarks of W. Gasz, *Geschichte der protestantischen Dogmatik,* I, pp. 164—167, comparing the exegetical techniques of Calov and Hugo Grotius.

⁵⁰ Cf. the statement of Johann Georg Neumann on philosophy as "a gift coming down from the Father of lights," "Praefatio" to Wilhelm Leyser, *Systema theticoexegeticum* (Wittenberg, 1690). Despite its title, Leyser's work is deductive rather than inductive in approach.

⁵¹ Karl Heim, *Das Gewiszheitsproblem in der systematischen Theologie bis Schleiermacher* (Leipzig, 1911) is a profound analysis of the problem in the Reformation, in Orthodoxy, and in Rationalism. For Chemnitz' view of certainty, cf. the passages from the *Examen* (Preuss ed., pp. 190—199), translated by H. E. Jacobs, "The Assurance of Faith," *Lutheran Quarterly*, I (1871), pp. 280—299.

⁵² See Arthur James Balfour, *A Defense of Philosophic Doubt* (New York, 1879), for a moving presentation by a great English statesman and thinker.

⁵³ The problem of certainty was of special concern to nineteenth-century "positive" Lutheran theology, represented by Ludwig Ihmels and Fr. Frank. Cf. also J. Gottschick, "Die Heilsgewiszheit des evangelischen Christen im Anschlusz an Luther," *Zeitschrift fuer Theologie und Kirche*, XIII (1903), pp. 349—435.

⁵⁴ Cf. the work of Ernst Troeltsch, *Der Historismus und seine Ueberwindung* (Berlin, 1925), for a detailed and profound analysis of the problem; as is often the case with Troeltsch, however, the diagnosis is far superior to the prescription. For an evaluation, cf. Otto Hintze, "Troeltsch und die Probleme des Historismus," *Historische Zeitschrift*, CXXXV (1926—1927), pp. 188—239.

⁵⁵ See the discussion of "Theologie und Gewiszheit," *Christliche Dogmatik*, I, pp. 123—147.

⁵⁶ His historical study of the question is referred to in note 51 above; for a more systematic treatment, cf. his essay, written during World War I, "Die Aufgabe der Apologetik in der Gegenwart," reprinted in his collected essays, *Glaube und Leben* (Berlin, 1926), pp. 157—180.

⁵⁷ David Hollaz, *Examen Theologiae Acroamaticae* (Rostock and Leipzig, 1722), I, 67, and I, 93.

⁵⁸ *Ibid.*, I, 127.

⁵⁹ The *testimonium Spiritus Sancti* (cf. Ch. IV, notes 5—8, below) was virtually equated with this assurance of the trustworthiness of the Scripture; see the passages cited in Johann Baier, *Compendium Theologiae Positivae*, edited by C. F. W. Walther (3 vols.; St. Louis, 1879), I, pp. 132—138.

⁶⁰ See also our discussion of Melanchthon's quest for certainty, Ch. II, notes 22—24, above.

⁶¹ Cf. notes 123 ff. below.

⁶² Gerhard's discussion, *Loci Theologici,* pp. 266—279, is learned, but still much less elaborate than those of his contemporaries and successors; cf. notes 98 ff. below.

⁶³ See the illuminating analysis of Orthodox language theory and semantics by Arnold Schleiff, "Sprachphilosophie und Inspirationstheorie im Denken des 17. Jahrhunderts," *Zeitschrift fuer Kirchengeschichte,* LVII (1938), pp. 133 to 152.

⁶⁴ Cf. Hans Engelland, *Melanchthon,* p. 197 ff.

⁶⁵ See Johann Dannhauer, *Hodosophia Christiana seu Theologia positiva* (3rd ed.; Leipzig, 1695), p. 186, an attempt to square the Augustinian formula "opera ad extra indivisa sunt" with the Incarnation.

⁶⁶ See the *Catechetischer Lehr-Grund* of Stephanus Pilarik (2nd ed.; Dresden, 1714), a work of 1290 pages of text, plus a lengthy introduction and a detailed index; cf. esp. pp. 483—486 on faith.

⁶⁷ On Luther's view of faith, see the essay of Wilhelm Pauck referred to in Ch. I, note 46, above, and Karl Holl, "Was verstand Luther unter Religion?" *Luther,* pp. 77—81.

⁶⁸ On assent, see my essay referred to in Ch. I, note 78, above, esp. Notes 27—49.

⁶⁹ In spite of some of its excesses, Albrecht Ritschl's posthumously published *Fides implicita* (Bonn, 1890), contains many valuable insights; on Luther, cf. p. 70.

⁷⁰ On Rathmann and the entire seventeenth-century development, cf. R. H. Gruetzmacher, *Wort und Geist. Eine Untersuchung zum Gnadenmittel des Wortes* (Leipzig, 1901), and the revision of Gruetzmacher's views in Otto Ritschl, *Dogmengeschichte des Protestantismus,* IV (Goettingen, 1927), pp. 157—172.

⁷¹ See below, notes 127—129 of this chapter.

⁷² *Examen,* I, 551, and I, 555.

⁷³ *Ibid.,* I, 519, and the demonstration of this view, I, 528 ff.

⁷⁴ *Ibid.,* I, 540.

⁷⁵ *Ibid.,* I, 518, and I, 76.

⁷⁶ *Ibid.,* I, 159, and I, 541.

⁷⁷ On methodology in religion and theology, contrasted with philosophy of religion, see the brilliant speculative presentation of Paul Tillich, "The Problem of Theological Method," *The Journal of Religion,* XXVII (1947), pp. 16—26.

78 Cf. Matthias Flacius Illyricus, *Clavis Scripturae Sacrae* (Jena, 1674), II, pp. 57—59, for a discussion of the analytic and synthetic method, plus the method of definition, with a table illustrating the differences.

79 See the complete and complex discussion of methodology by Abraham Calov, *Scripta philosophica* (Wittenberg, 1673), p. 1036 ff.

80 Professor Pieper points out, *Christliche Dogmatik,* I, pp. 172—182, that either method can be used in a completely orthodox presentation.

81 W. Gasz, *Geschichte der protestantischen Dogmatik,* I, pp. 128—130, refutes the claim that the synthetic method is characteristically Reformed, while the analytic is more suited to Lutheran theology.

82 See Ch. II, notes 46—50, above.

83 Johann Baier, *Compendium Theologiae Positivae* (see note 59 above); David Hollaz, *Examen Theologiae Acroamaticae* (see note 57 above). These two works also form an excellent case study for the relationship of Orthodoxy to Pietism.

84 See Ch. III, notes 93—97, below.

85 In his discussion of methodology referred to in note 80 above, Professor Pieper also remarks that the analytic method is more suited to speculative discussion than is the synthetic: *Christliche Dogmatik,* I, p. 177.

86 Nels F. S. Ferré, *Faith and Reason,* pp. 1—37, points to Whitehead's work in this area and attempts to employ some of Whitehead's insights for the determination of the respective areas of religion, science, and philosophy.

87 Cf. the brief but helpful discussion of Pierre Albert Duhamel, "The Logic and Rhetoric of Peter Ramus," *Modern Philology,* XLVI (1948—1949), pp. 163—171.

88 Perry Miller's thorough study of *Orthodoxy in Massachusetts* is an interpretation of the Ramist elements in the type of Calvinism which the Puritans brought from Europe and developed in America.

89 See the list of Ramus' writings in Petersen, *op. cit.,* p. 127, note 1, and the discussion of Ramus' theories, pp. 127—143.

90 On the Lutheran attitude, cf. Weber, *op. cit.,* pp. 21—27.

91 E. Schlee, *Der Streit des Daniel Hofmann ueber das Verhaeltnis der Philosophie zur Theologie* (Marburg, 1862).

92 For the positive influence of Ramism, see Weber, *op. cit.,* pp. 22—24.

93 Aristotle's most precise discussion of cause is in the *Metaphysics,* Book V, Ch. 2, *The Basic Works of Aristotle,* pp. 752—754.

94 See the Index to Walther's edition of Baier's *Compendium*, compiled by Theodor Buenger (Saint Louis, 1909), p. 18, *sub voce* "causa," for a catalog of the various *causae* of Orthodox metaphysics.

95 Johann Gerhard, *Loci Theologici*, I, p. 495, in a discussion of whether the Holy Spirit can properly be called the Father of Christ.

96 It is enlightening to compare the causes discussed by seventeenth-century Aristotelians (see note 94) with Aristotle's own discussion (see note 93). In another passage Aristotle lists the four causes and comments: "This, then, perhaps exhausts the number of ways in which the term cause is used," *Physics*, Book II, Ch. 3, *Basic Works*, pp. 240—241.

97 So, for example, by Hollaz, "Locus de Praedestinatione," *Examen*, II, pp. 28—39, with a careful distinction between two forms of the *causa efficiens* and two forms of the *causa impulsiva*.

98 Ernst Troeltsch, *Vernunft und Offenbarung bei Johann Gerhard und Melanchthon. Untersuchung zur Geschichte der altprotestantischen Theologie* (Goettingen, 1891).

99 Werner Elert has a brief but excellent summary in his *Morphologie des Luthertums*, I, pp. 44—52. Hans Emil Weber, *Reformation, Orthodoxie und Rationalismus*, I, *Von der Reformation zur Orthodoxie* (Guetersloh, 1937), pp. 174—177, presents an interesting critique of Troeltsch's interpretation of Melanchthon; Volume II would have treated Gerhard, where, it seems to me, Troeltsch's thesis is even more vulnerable. Nevertheless, a great deal of research remains to be done on this important problem.

100 In a brief essay on "Natural Theology in David Hollaz," *Concordia Theological Monthly*, XVII (1947), pp. 253—263, I have analyzed Hollaz' views on natural knowledge. Much of the material that follows here is either in or behind that essay. Cf. p. 255, note 12 of the essay for additional seventeenth-century works on the subject.

101 Hollaz, *Examen*, I, 512.

102 *Ibid.*, I, 48.

103 *Ibid.*, I, 575.

104 *Ibid.*, I, 214.

105 *Ibid.*, I, 209.

106 *Ibid.*, I, 216; commenting on this passage, Professor Pieper suggests that "wir werden Hollaz recht geben muessen," *Christliche Dogmatik* I, p. 447, note 1203.

107 Hollaz, *Examen*, I, 66.

108 *Ibid.*, I, 379.

109 *Ibid.*, I, 129.

110 *Ibid.*, II, 460.

111 *Ibid.*, I, 388—389.

112 Cf. on this question Thomas Aquinas in the Summa Theologica, Q. 46, *The Basic Writings of Saint Thomas Aquinas*, I, pp. 447—457. See the comments of Richard McKeon, "Aristotelianism in Western Christianity" in *Environmental Factors in Christian History* (Chicago, 1939), p. 220 ff.

113 Hollaz, *Examen*, I, 391—393.

114 *Ibid.*, II, 721.

115 Cf. J. G. Walch, *Historische und Theologische Einleitung in die Religions-Streitigkeiten der Evangelisch-Lutherischen Kirche* (Jena, 17—), II, pp. 76—91; V, pp. 159—162.

116 Hollaz, *Examen*, I, 167.

117 *Ibid.*, I, 174; I, 203. See the brief note on Hollaz and the "theologia irregenitorum" in Pieper, *Christliche Dogmatik*, I, pp. 175—176, note 584.

118 See the work of Troeltsch, referred to in note 98 above, and of Elert, referred to in note 99; also Baier, *Compendium* (Walther edition), I, pp. 5—30, for the lengths to which the Orthodox discussions of natural theology sometimes went.

119 Hollaz, *Examen*, I, 30.

120 *Ibid.*, I, 31; on the oneness of truth, cf. Karl Heim, "Zur Geschichte des Satzes von der doppelten Wahrheit," *Glaube und Leben*, pp. 73—97.

121 Hollaz, *Examen*, I, 78; cf. the discussion of Johann Gerhard, "Disputatio de Mysterio Sacrosanctae et Individuae Trinitatis," in his *Disputationes Isagogicae* (Jena, 1645), pp. 184—185.

122 Hollaz, *Examen*, I, 375.

123 Gustaf Aulén, *Den kristna gudsbilden*, summarized by Carlson, *The Reinterpretation of Luther*, pp. 141—150.

124 Cf. Rudolf Otto's discussion of "The Numinous in Luther," *The Idea of the Holy*, pp. 97—112.

125 Anders Nygren, *Agape and Eros*, Part II, p. 511 ff.

126 Cf. Gustaf Aulén, *The Faith of the Christian Church*, pp. 139—141, on "the wrath of love."

[127] ". . . non potest homo naturaliter velle deum esse deum, immo vellet se esse deum et deum non esse deum," "Contra scholasticam theologiam," *WA* I, 225.

[128] Hollaz, *Examen,* I, 531—532.

[129] On Hollaz' view of sin in connection with his doctrine of the Atonement, cf. Ivar Holm, *Dogmhistoriska Studier till Hollazius,* I, *Trostankarna i raettfaerdiggoerelselaeran* (Lund, 1907), pp. 28—30.

[130] See the comments of T. A. Kantonen in his essay "God," in E. C. Fendt (ed.), *What Lutherans Are Thinking* (Columbus, 1947), pp. 134—135.

[131] On the analogy of Being, see the extremely sympathetic remarks of Gilbert Chesterton, *Saint Thomas Aquinas* (New York, 1933), pp. 184—188.

[132] Elert's discussion of "Natuerliche Theologie," *Morphologie des Luthertums,* I (Muenchen, 1931), pp. 44—52, seeks to evaluate the significance of this change for later Lutheran development.

[133] "Ist die Absolution kategorisch oder hypothetisch zu sprechen?" *Lehre und Wehre,* XXII (1876), p. 193; see the discussion of Pieper, *Christliche Dogmatik,* II, p. 652.

[134] Even Johann Gerhard, in whom the evangelical intentions of the Reformation find articulation more clearly than in most of the other dogmaticians, involved himself in this, so that in his "Locus de Deo" he can refer to Aristotle simply as "Philosophus," *Loci Theologici,* I, p. 268.

[135] See Whitehead's critique of metaphysical doctrines of God, including that of Aristotle, *Science and the Modern World* (New York, 1926), pp. 249—258.

[136] Blaise Pascal, *Pensées sur la Religion,* translated by W. F. Trotter (Modern Library Edition; New York, 1941), No. 555, pp. 180-183.

[137] See note 147 below.

[138] *Concordia Triglotta,* pp. 1107—1149. It is noteworthy that so many of the quotations are taken from Eastern rather than from Western Fathers.

[139] See the careful discussion of ancient Christology by Emil Brunner, *The Mediator,* translated by Olive Wyon (Philadelphia, 1947), pp. 249—264, correcting the interpretations of the Ancient Church by Ritschl and Harnack and assessing more accurately than they the respective contributions of Christian and Greek elements in the patristic doctrine of Christ.

[140] Cf. Emil Brunner, *Man in Revolt,* pp. 362—363, note 1.

[141] See some representative quotations on this question in Baier, *Compendium,* II, pp. 100—102; cf. also Martin Chemnitz, *Loci,* I, p. 236, for a very cautious statement; and the disputation of Matthaeus Elieser Wendius, *Nova de animae humanae propagatione sententia* (Wittenberg, 1712).

142 *The Basic Works of Aristotle,* edited by Richard McKeon, pp. 535—625.

143 The work is available only in manuscript; cf. Samuel Štephan Osusky, "M. Hlaváč-Kephalides: De Pluralitate Animarum" in *Sborník na počest Jozefa Škultétyho* (Turčiansky Sväty Martin, 1933), pp. 216—222.

144 The outstanding exposition of Lutheran Christology and one of the truly masterful theological works of the second generation of Lutheran theology is Martin Chemnitz, *De duabus naturis in Christo, de hypostatica earum unione,* I have used the edition of Leipzig, 1600.

145 This was the topic of a controversy in which Joachim Lütkemann was involved; see the detailed and almost tedious account of Quenstedt, *Theologia didactico-polemica sive systema theologiae* (Wittenberg, 1696), II, pp. 594 ff.

146 Cf. Aegidius Hunnius, *De persona Christi, eiusque ad dextram Dei sedentis divina majestate* (Franckfort, 1590), p. 27: "tristis est anima mea, esque ad mortem: Quod de Divinitate explicari nequit, quippe quae nec tristitiae . . . capax est . . . Proinde veram quoque animam assumpsit: neque vero eam vegetativam duntaxat et sensitivam, sed rationalem spiritum." The latter distinction of the vegetative, sensitive, and rational soul is taken from Aristotle.

147 To my knowledge, there is no such investigation; in the preface to his scholarly work, *Coena Domini. Eine Untersuchung zur altlutherischen Abendmahlslehre* (München, 1937), Helmut Gollwitzer promised a similarly thorough study of Lutheran Christology, but he was apparently prevented by the war from completing this project. The circumstance noted above (note 138) of the prominence of the Eastern Fathers in the *Catalogus testimoniorum* would suggest that the Lutheran formulation might stand in continuity with Chalcedon rather than with the Christological work of the scholastics.

148 See Balthasar Meisner's critique of the Reformed conception of space in his *Philosophia sobria,* I, pp. 676—681.

149 Cf. the treatise "Das diese wort Christi (Das ist mein leib etce) noch fest stehen widder die Schwermegeister," *WA* XXIII, 143 and *passim;* Johann Gerhard, *Loci Theologici,* I, pp. 552-561.

150 Quoted in Pieper, *Christliche Dogmatik,* II, p. 205.

151 *De duabus naturis,* p. 191 and *passim.*

152 Balthasar Meisner, *Philosophia sobria,* I, p. 673.

153 See Ch. IV, note 129, below.

154 For a typical conception of *substantia* in the Age of Orthodoxy, cf. Abraham Calov, *Scripta philosophica, Metaphysica divina,* II, p. 155.

155 See Ch. IV, notes 123 ff., below.

[156] Neither Roman Catholicism nor Calvinism could free itself from the space-bound physics and metaphysics of Aristotle; both the Catholic and the Reformed doctrines of the Lord's Supper are predicated on the assumption that space is real and that even Christ has to conform Himself to space, even if miraculously, to be present in the Sacrament.

[157] See note 34 above; on Meisner, cf. August Tholuck, *Der Geist der lutherischen Theologen Wittenbergs im Verlaufe des 17. Jahrhunderts* (Hamburg, 1852), pp. 14—37.

[158] *Philosophia sobria*, II, p. 482.

[159] Cf. the statement of the Apology, *Concordia Triglotta*, p. 233.

[160] *Philosophia sobria*, I, pp. 122—124.

[161] The notion of *quidditas* underlies the very word "substance" and serves to infect every theology in which a metaphysic of substance plays a part. It is difficult to understand how the term "substance" can be fitted into any metaphysic that seeks to take account of the results of modern physics.

[162] On the object-subject antithesis, see our discussion in Ch. I, notes 78—80.

[163] David Hume, *An Enquiry Concerning Human Understanding*, in Edwin Burtt (ed.), *The English Philosophers from Bacon to Mill* (New York, 1939), pp. 585—689, esp. Section VII, "Of the Idea of Necessary Connection," pp. 620 to 633. See also Bertrand Russell's essay "On the Notion of Cause," *Mysticism and Logic* (New York, 1929), pp. 180—208.

[164] See Ch. IV, notes 125—127, below.

[165] Adolf Hult has tried to develop Lutheran theological insights into an interpretation of history in his pamphlet *The Theology of History* (Rock Island, 1940), but many problems are left unanswered.

[166] Cf. Reinhold Niebuhr, *The Nature and Destiny of Man*, II, *Human Destiny*, pp. 35—67, esp. pp. 65—66, on God's hiddenness in history.

[167] The naiveté to which I refer is the tendency on the part of men like Zwingli and Erasmus to imagine that they could leap back to the period of the New Testament without taking account of the intervening centuries. Much of modern Fundamentalism has fallen into the same unhistorical fallacy and has sought to identify this attitude with the Christian doctrine of the Word of God.

[168] Cf. Ch. IV, notes 73—80, below for Leibniz' attempt.

[169] Cf. Peter Meinhold, "Luthers philosophische und geschichtstheologische Gedanken," *Blätter für deutsche Philosophie*, X (1936), p. 56 ff.

[170] At least part of the reason is the static conception of both nature and society that Orthodoxy developed under Aristotelian influence. When history is thought of statically, no evangelical and dynamic theology of history is possible.

NOTES TO CHAPTER IV

1 The best study of Quenstedt known to me is Max Koch, *Der ordo salutis in der alt-lutherischen Dogmatik* (Berlin, 1899), pp. 5—108, though his discussion is marred by his theological bias.

2 Thus, for example, Quenstedt devoted consideration to the problem of whether justification by faith is an analytic or a synthetic judgment in the mind of God; *Theologia didactico-polemica,* III, 585.

3 August Tholuck, *Lebenszeugen der lutherischen Kirche aus allen Ständen vor und während des dreiszigjährigen Krieges* (Berlin, 1859), discusses some of the century's outstanding pastors, but concentrates upon its theologians, who were the true princes of the Church.

4 On the fate of Orthodoxy during the eighteenth century, see Theodor Wotschke, "Die Nöte der Orthodoxie in Wittenberg," *Zeitschrift für Kirchengeschichte,* LII, (1933), pp. 286—304.

5 Johann Gerhard, "Locus de Justificatione per Fidem," *Loci Theologici,* III, pp. 373—375.

6 David Hollaz, *Examen Theologiae Acroamaticae,* I, pp. 220—231.

7 Wilhelm Walther, *Das Zeugnisz des heiligen Geistes nach Luther und nach moderner Schwärmerei* (Leipzig, 1899), a sample of the author's ability to make Reformation theology intelligible to modern men.

8 See the passages cited in Baier's *Compendium,* I, pp. 132—138, and Ch. III, note 59, above.

9 Kenneth Scott Latourette, *A History of the Expansion of Christianity,* III, *Three Centuries of Advance* (New York, 1939), pp. 25—27.

10 *Morphologie des Luthertums,* I, pp. 336—344.

11 See some instances of the honoraria paid for polemical writings in August Tholuck, *Der Geist der lutherischen Theologen Wittenbergs im Verlaufe des 17. Jahrhunderts* (Hamburg, 1852), pp. 30—37.

12 Gerhard, "Locus de Ecclesia," *Loci Theologici,* V, p. 426.

13 Cf. Elert, *Morphologie,* II, pp. 23—37, on the ethical impact of the Reformation, including an examination of the contrast between Luther and Melanchthon.

14 Renatus Hupfeld, *Die Ethik Johann Gerhards* (Berlin, 1908).

15 *Ibid.,* pp. 202—203, especially the footnote, and *passim.*

16 See Gerhard's discussion of *caritas, Loci Theologici,* III, p. 404 ff., and its application to political life, *ibid.,* VI, pp. 390—391.

17 Cf. Christian Luthardt, *Geschichte der christlichen Ethik*, II, (Leipzig, 1893), pp. 187—192, on this separation in Calixtus.

18 Hans Leube's *Die Reformideen in der deutschen lutherischen Kirche zur Zeit der Orthodoxie* (1924) is an attempt to correct the excesses of interpretations like those of Tholuk and to show that there was always an ethically sensitive element in Orthodox Lutheranism. In general, it seems to me, the thesis stands; but on the problem of the interrelations of Lutheranism and philosophy the amount of dissatisfied stirring seems to have been slight.

19 Thus, W. Gasz, *Geschichte der protestantischen Dogmatik*, still the standard work on the subject, and August Tholuck's *Der Geist der lutherischen Theologen Wittenbergs* can be read without any knowledge that the Thirty Years' War almost ruined Germany.

20 Cf. Veit Valentin, *The German People*, pp. 213—217, for a balanced evaluation of the effect of the War upon German population and life.

21 Above all, of course, in Paul Gerhardt, but he was by no means the only one; on Heermann von Köben, cf. Tholuck, *Lebenszeugen*, pp. 307—313.

22 See J. G. Walch, *Historische und Theologische Einleitung in die Religions-Streitigkeiten der Evangelisch-Lutherischen Kirche*, V, pp 938—973, on the chiliasm of the time.

23 The extent to which Jakob Böhme revived some of Luther's neglected views and the extent to which he perverted them is discussed in full by Heinrich Bornkamm, *Luther und Böhme* (Bonn, 1925).

24 J. G. Walch, *op cit.*, V, pp. 973—998, on the controversies stirred by Arnold's work.

25 Erich Seeberg, *Gottfried Arnold, die Wissenschaft und die Mystik seiner Zeit. Studie zur Historiographie und zur Mystik* (Meerane i. Sa., 1923) carefully assesses Arnold's debt to earlier mystical and spiritualistic thinkers, as well as his influence on those who followed.

26 Albrecht Ritschl's monumental *Geschichte des Pietismus* (3 vols.; Bonn, 1880—1886) is still the standard work on Pietism. Although my presentation owes much to Ritschl's work, the many blind spots in his book make the composition of a new history of Pietism a prime need in contemporary research in the history of Protestantism.

27 This is, it seems to me, one of the areas Ritschl ignores. Though source material would be difficult to find, a careful examination of assorted parishes in Germany during the two centuries following the Reformation would be necessary in any attempt to evaluate the conditions that made Pietism possible.

28 Cf. Valentin, *op cit.*, pp. 259—263, on German culture and life in the early eighteenth century.

[29] See, for example, Johann Gerhard, *Homiliae Sacrae in pericopas evangeliorum dominicalium et praecipuorum totius anni festorum,* III (Jena, 1634), pp. 911—921, on love for God. And Gerhard's preaching is still much better than that of twenty-five and fifty years later! One example of evangelical preaching is Valerius Herberger, whose sermons and hymns were Christ-centered; cf. Tholuck, *Lebenszeugen,* pp. 282—291.

[30] The popular biography by Marie E. Richard, *Philip Jacob Spener and His Work* (Philadelphia, 1897), though by no means a scholarly production, can still be read with much profit.

[31] On the relationship of Pietist mysticism to the Orthodox *unio mystica,* cf. Ritschl, *Geschichte des Pietismus,* II, p. 29 ff., and Koch, op. cit., p. 140, note 1; on the relation of the *unio mystica* to Luther, see my essay "The Structure of Luther's Piety," pp. 19—20, and the statement cited there from Heinrich Scholz, "Fruitio Dei," appendix to *Glaube und Unglaube in der Weltgeschichte: Ein Kommentar zu Augustins De Civitate Dei* (Leipzig, 1911), p. 226.

[32] But see note 26 above on the need for more research on Pietism.

[33] Latourette, *op. cit.,* pp. 46—48.

[34] See Ch. III, note 20, above.

[35] Cf. Paul Henry Lang, *Music in Western Civilization* (New York, 1941), pp. 468—475.

[36] K. S. Pinson, *Pietism as a Factor in the Rise of German Nationalism* (New York, 1934).

[37] J. G. Walch, *op. cit.,* II, pp. 541—543, on some of the Pietists' views on philosophy.

[38] On some of the opposition between Pietism and philosophy, see the essay of Eduard Zeller on Wolff referred to in note 88 below.

[39] J. G. Walch, *Historiche und Theologische Einleitung in die Religions-Streitigkeiten der Evangelisch-Lutherischen Kirche,* II, pp. 20—75, for a listing of the chief books involved in the controversy.

[40] G. Vuernsdorf, *Osiandrismus in pietismo renatus* (Wittenberg, n. d.); the treatise is preserved in the library of Valparaiso University.

[41] Johann Albert Bengel, *Gnomon Novi Testamenti,* edited by Paul Steudel (Stuttgart, 1891), was the first piece of profound New Testament scholarship to come out of Lutheranism for a long time; cf. Ch. III, note 48, above.

[42] See my essay "Natural Theology in David Hollaz," p. 255.

[43] It is an interesting phenomenon of theological history that conservative and liberal theologians are agreed on this point; Ritschl's interpretation (see note 26 above) is substantiated by the explanation current in many conservative Lutheran seminaries and books.

[44] Cf. Walch, *op. cit.*, II, pp. 537—643, for the Pietist critique of rationalistic Orthodox metaphysics.

[45] Emil Brunner, *The Divine-Human Encounter,* p. 34.

[46] See the shrewd comments of Arthur James Balfour, *The Foundations of Belief* (New York, 1895), pp. 182—189, on "Rationalistic Orthodoxy."

[47] Ch. III, notes 62—65, above.

[48] Ch. II, notes 37—39, above.

[49] Ch. III, notes 115—117, above.

[50] "Ernesti was, perhaps, the first to formulate with perfect clearness the principle which has been much discussed in our own day, 'that the verbal sense of Scripture must be determined in the same way in which we ascertain that of other books,'" Frederic W. Farrar, *History of Interpretation* (New York, 1886), p. 402.

[51] John F. Hurst, *History of Rationalism* (9th ed.; New York, n. d.), p. 127.

[52] Cf. Erich Schmidt, *Lessing. Geschichte seines Lebens und seiner Schriften* (2 vols., 4th ed.; Berlin, 1923), II, pp. 208—209.

[53] *Ibid.,* p. 209 ff. on this attempt and Semler's relation to it.

[54] Hurst's entire discussion, *op. cit.,* pp. 125—143, covers the history of Rationalism's attempt to come to terms with these proofs.

[55] Kuno Fischer, *Geschichte der neuern Philosophie,* II, *Gottfried Wilhelm Leibniz* (3rd ed.; Heidelberg, 1889), is still indispensable; the handiest English summary is Herbert Wildon Carr, *Leibniz* (Boston, 1929); see also the brilliant sketch by Wilhelm Dilthey, "Leibniz und sein Zeitalter," *Gesammelte Schriften,* III, (Leipzig, 1927), pp. 1—80.

[56] For a Whiteheadian analysis of Leibniz, cf. Charles Hartshorne, "Leibniz' Greatest Discovery," *Journal of the History of Ideas,* VII, (1946), pp. 411—421; see also Professor Hartshorne's *The Divine Relativity* (New Haven, 1948), p. 30.

[57] The entire issue of the *Journal of the History of Ideas* referred to in the previous note is devoted to Leibniz; cf. especially William E. Sheldon, "Leibniz' Message to Us," pp. 385—396.

[58] The closest thing we have to such an evaluation is still the work of A. Pichler, *Die Theologie des Leibniz* (2 vols.; München, 1869).

[59] William Turner's article on Leibniz in *The Catholic Encyclopedia,* IX, pp. 134—138, discusses Leibniz' attitude toward Catholicism, but no longer makes the claim that he embraced Roman Catholicism.

[60] See the suggestive comments of Karl Holl, "Die Kulturbedeutung der Reformation," *Luther,* pp. 530—531.

[61] Of all the medieval thinkers, Nicholas of Cusa was perhaps most influential in Leibniz; cf. the old but still useful study of R. Zimmermann, *Der Kardinal Nikolaus von Kues als Vorläufer Leibnitz's* (Weimar, 1852).

[62] Petersen, *Geschichte der aristotelischen Philosophie im protestantischen Deutschland*, p. 341.

[63] "Disputatio metaphysica de principio individui," *Sämtliche Schriften und Briefe, Philosophische Schriften*, I (Darmstadt, 1930), pp. 11—19.

[64] Cf. H. W. Carr, *The Monadology of Leibniz, with an Introduction, Commentary, and Supplementary Essays* (London, 1930) for the text and a complete discussion of the Monadologie.

[65] See representative passages referred to by Emil Weber, *Die philosophische Scholastik des deutschen Protestantismus*, p. 3, note 2.

[66] Cf. Ch. III, note 143, above.

[67] Carr, *Leibniz*, pp. 73—82.

[68] Cf. Ch. III, notes 148—163.

[69] See Petersen's brief discussion of causality, *op. cit.*, p. 373.

[70] Weber, *op. cit.*, pp. 3—4, note 4.

[71] *Ibid.*

[72] On the influence of Bruno and others upon Leibniz' monadology, see Carr's detailed treatment, referred to in note 64 above.

[73] *Essais de Théodicée sur la bonté de Dieu, la liberté de l'homme et l'origine du mal* in G. M. Duncan's translation (New Haven, 1890).

[74] Cf. Gerhard Stammler, *Leibniz* (München, 1930), p. 129 ff. on the theology of Leibniz.

[75] See Johann Eduard Erdmann, *Grundriss der Geschichte der Philosophie* (4th ed.; Berlin, 1896), II, pp. 161—179, on Leibniz' critique of Descartes.

[76] Leibniz' last treatise, published in 1714, was entitled *Principes de la nature et la grace, fondés en raison.*

[77] Werner Elert has pointed out, *Morphologie*, I, p. 416 ff., that Leibniz' solution of the problem of evil is artificial because of his failure to recognize the tension between what must be done and what ought to be done.

[78] But see the penetrating comments of Immanuel Kant's brief analysis, "Ueber das Misslingen aller philosophischen Versuche in der Theodicee" (1791) in *Sämmtliche Werke*, edited by G. Hartenstein, VI (Leipzig, 1868), pp. 77 to 93.

[79] Alfred Weber, *History of Philosophy*, translated by Frank Thilly (New York, 1925), p. 295.

[80] On some of these interrelations cf. the discussion of Ernst Troeltsch, "Leibniz und die Anfänge des Pietismus," *Gesammelte Schriften*, IV (Tübingen, 1925), pp. 488—531; see also Petersen's summary of Aristotle's influence upon Leibniz, *op. cit.*, pp. 340—380.

[81] For an evaluation of Leibniz in terms of modern physics, cf. Ulrich Fürle, *Ueber die Beziehung von Leibnizens System zum modernen physikalischen Weltbild* (Breslau, 1934).

[82] On Leibniz' relation to his time, cf. the remarks of Karl Barth, *Die protestantische Theologie im 19. Jahrhundert* (Zurich, 1847), pp. 16—59.

[83] The best brief modern analysis of Wolff's view of philosophy known to me is the essay by Hans Lüthje, "Christian Wolff's Philosophiebegriff," *Kant-Studien*, XXX (1925).

[84] See the summary statement of Pierre Gaxotte, *Frederick the Great*, translated by R. A. Bell (New Haven, 1942), pp. 146—147: "Wolff was obscure and pedestrian. . . . He endowed the philosophy of Leibniz with all the strictness of a mathematical chain of reasoning: he wanted all the propositions of his system to be deduced the one from the other with demonstrative certainty."

[85] Cf. H. Droysen, *Friedrich-Wilhelm, Friedrich der Grosse und der Philosoph Christian Wolff*, No. 23 of "Forschungen zur brandenburgischen und preussischen Geschichte" (Leipzig, 1910), on Wolff's difficulties with the political authorities because of his opposition to Orthodox theology.

[86] Quoted in Christian Luthardt, *Kompendium der Dogmatik* (3rd ed.; Leipzig, 1868), p. 51.

[87] See the detailed summary of Wolff's philosophy in Erdmann, *op. cit.*, II, pp. 197—212, and the discussion of Wolff's impact upon his time, *ibid.*, p. 212 ff.

[88] Cf. Eduard Zeller, "Wolff's Vertreibung aus Halle. Der Kampf des Pietismus mit der Philosophie," in his *Vorträge und Abhandlungen* (2nd ed.; Leipzig, 1875).

[89] On the relation of the movements in England and France, cf. N. L. Torrey, *Voltaire and the English Deists* (New Haven, 1930).

[90] See J. Musaeus' *De luminis naturae insufficientia contra H. Cherbury*, preserved in the Pritzlaff Memorial Library of Concordia Seminary, for a Lutheran defense of revelation against Deism.

[91] Cf. Robert Shafer, "Religious Thought in England in the XVIIth and XVIIIth Centuries," in *Christianity and Naturalism. Essays in Criticism* (New Haven, 1926), pp. 1—33.

[92] Carl L. Becker, *The Heavenly City of the Eighteenth-Century Philosophers* (New Haven, 1947), esp. the summary statement, pp. 48—49.

93 See the penetrating study of these interrelations by W. Langer, *Friedrich der Grosse und die geistige Welt Frankreichs* (Hamburg, 1932) for an assessment of the prestige of French thought in Germany.

94 On the contacts between Frederick and Voltaire, see *Letters of Voltaire and Frederick the Great,* translated and edited by Richard Addington (London, 1927).

95 Bogdan Krieger, *Frederick the Great and His Books* (New York, 1913), is an interpretation of the intellectual interests of Frederick in the light of his library.

96 Cf. Pierre Gaxotte, *op. cit.,* pp. 288—297.

97 H. Schmid, *Die Theologie Semlers* (Erlangen, 1858), is still as good a study as is available of Semler's thought.

98 On Semler's contemporaries and their interest in the same problems, see notes 50—54 above.

99 See the brief and touching description of the close of his life by Fr. Aug. Wolf, *Ueber Herrn Semlers letzte Lebenstage* (Halle, 1791).

100 In their study of isagogics the theologians of the seventeenth century rarely went far beyond the scholarly investigations of Martin Chemnitz, *Examen Concilii Tridentini* (Preuss ed.), pp. 21—61.

101 Barth, *Die protestantische Theologie,* pp. 142—152.

102 Cf. Ch. III, notes 115—117, on the "theologia irregenitorum."

103 See the quotations on the New Testament offered in Schmid, *op. cit.,* pp. 93—100.

104 On Semler, see also the statements of Farrar, *op. cit.,* pp. 402—405.

105 The clearest statement of his position on theology and philosophy is in his "Einleitung in die dogmatische Gottesgelehrsamkeit," running through all three volumes of Siegmund Jacob Baumgarten, *Evangelische Glaubenslehre* (Halle, 1760), II, pp. 24—25.

106 Cf. the comments of Albert Schweitzer, *The Quest of the Historical Jesus,* translated by W. Montgomery (London, 1911), pp. 25—26, on Semler's inauguration of a "Yes, but theology."

107 On Lessing, see the detailed biography by Erich Schmidt, *Lessing. Geschichte seines Lebens und seiner Schriften* (4th ed., 2 vols.; Berlin, 1923).

108 Gottfried Fittbogen, *Die Religion Lessings* (Leipzig, 1923), has summarized his theological views; on his early religious development, see Matthijs Jolles, "Das religiöse Jugendbekenntnis Lessings" in Arnold Bergsträsser (ed.), *Deutsche Beiträge zur geistigen Ueberlieferung,* pp. 115—133.

109 Johann Gottfried Lessing, *Vindiciae reformationis Lutheri a nonnullis novatorum praejudiciis* (Wittenberg, 1717). The work is in the library of Valparaiso University.

110 There is a summary of Lessing's philosophy of religion in H. B. Garland, *Lessing. The Founder of Modern German Literature* (Cambridge, 1937), pp. 151—186; the religious theories embodied in *Nathan der Weise* are discussed, pp. 179—186.

111 Schmidt, *op cit.*, II, pp. 165—295, has given a careful account of Lessing's conflict with the theologians.

112 On Lessing's relation to the German Enlightenment, cf. Ernest Kretzschmar, *Ueber das Verhältnis Lessings in seiner "Erziehung des Menschengeschlechts" zur deutschen Aufklärung* (Borna-Leipzig, 1904).

113 See Barth's chapter on Lessing, *Die protestantische Theologie*, pp. 208 to 236.

114 Friedrich Paulsen, *Immanuel Kant. Sein Leben und seine Lehre* (5th ed.; Stuttgart, n. d.), pp. 30—32.

115 Cf. R. M. Wenley, *Kant and his Philosophical Revolution* (New York, 1910), pp. 65—66.

116 See Ludwig Ernst Borowski, *Darstellung des Lebens und Charakters Immanuel Kants* in *Immanuel Kant. Sein Leben in Darstellungen von Zeitgenossen* (Berlin, 1912), p. 21; as indicated in note 2, Kant himself approved Borowski's statement in manuscript form.

117 *Ibid.*, pp. 21—22.

118 See Wenley's characterization of Schultz, *op. cit.*, p. 62 ff.

119 Borowski, *op. cit.*, p. 25, note 1, presents some interesting data on Kant's desire to enter the ministry — a passage which Kant excised from Borowski's biography.

120 Cf. Paulsen, *op. cit.*, pp. 39—42, for an evaluation of Kant's study in the physical sciences.

121 See Kant's prize essay, "Welches sind die wirklichen Fortschritte, die die Metaphysik seit Leibnitz's und Wolff's Zeiten in Deutschland gemacht hat?", *Sämmtliche Werke*, VIII, pp. 519—592.

122 Karl Barth, *Die protestantische Theologie*, pp. 237—278.

123 Colossians 3:3.

124 See, in general, the Gifford Lectures of Richard Kroner, *The Primacy of Faith* (New York, 1943), esp. Chapter II on "Kant's Critique of Natural Theology," pp. 24—45, for a presentation that is both Christian in its concern and philosophical in its orientation.

[125] *Critique of Pure Reason,* translated by J. M. D. Meiklejohn (New York, 1901), pp. 438—476.

[126] Cf. Professor Stöckhardt's polemic against those who would make of the natural knowledge taught by Paul in Rom. 1:20 "a kind of means of grace which brings at least some men to God or closer to God," *Commentar über den Brief Pauli an die Römer* (St. Louis, 1907), p. 54. See also Bishop Nygren's comments *sub loco* in his *Commentary on Romans,* tr. by Carl C. Rasmussen (Philadelphia, 1949), pp. 102—109, pointing out the two current misinterpretations of this passage: some interpreters take Rom. 1:20 as an excuse to construct a theology of pure reason; others forget that there is a revelation of God in the Creation. It is against the former that Kant's critique is directed.

[127] *Critique of Pure Reason,* p. 473.

[128] Ch. III, notes 148—152.

[129] *Critique of Pure Reason,* pp. 65—89.

[130] For some of Luther's thinking about this problem, see Johann Haar, *Initium Creaturae Dei* (Gütersloh, 1939), pp. 22—27.

[131] Cf. Werner Elert, *Morphologie des Luthertums,* I, pp. 360—361.

[132] On this and related problems in Luther, cf. also Holl, "Was verstand Luther unter Religion?", *Luther,* p. 81.

[133] Elert, *loc. cit.*

[134] H. J. Paton, *The Categorical Imperative. A Study in Kant's Moral Philosophy* (Chicago, 1948), p. 196.

[135] *Die Religion innerhalb der Grenzen der blosen Vernunft* (1793), *Werke,* VI, p. 253, with a detailed exposition in the accompanying footnote.

[136] On Kant's philosophy of religion, cf. the summary by A. Hazard Dakin, "Kant and Religion," in George Tapley Whitney and David F. Bowers (ed.), *The Heritage of Kant* (Princeton, 1939), pp. 405—420.

[137] With characteristic penetration, Ernst Troeltsch has analyzed *Religion within the Limits of Reason Alone* as a compromise between rationalism and the faith of the Church: "Das Historische in Kants Religionsphilosophie," *Kant-Studien,* IX, (1904), pp. 21—154.

[138] Cf. Karl Holl, "Der Neubau der Sittlichkeit," *Luther,* pp. 259—263, on Luther's concept of *Beruf;* see also Valentin, *The German People,* p. 298, on "the junction of Kant's ethos, Luther's idea of vocation, and the Prussian view of the state" in German constitutionalism.

[139] Carl Schneider, "Das Synthetische in der religiösen Erkenntnis" in Robert Jelke (ed.), *Das Erbe Martin Luthers und die gegenwärtige Forschung,* p. 199, note 1.

[140] T. A. Kantonen, *Resurgence of the Gospel* (Philadelphia, 1948), p. 61.

[141] The discussion of radical evil appears in *Die Religion innerhalb der Grenzen der blosen Vernunft, Werke,* VI, pp. 113—147.

[142] Paul Arthur Schilpp, *Kant's Pre-Critical Ethics* (Evanston, 1938); on his debt to Pietism, cf. esp. pp. 49—51, also the summary statement, p. 169: "Contrary to the usual interpretation and estimate of this influence as a hindrance, Kant's early Pietism gave him not only a supreme regard for the worth of human personality and for the values inherent in social relationship, but also the initial impetus toward a dynamic instead of a static interpretation of human life and experience."

[143] Reinhold Niebuhr, *The Nature and Destiny of Man* (New York, 1943), I, *Human Nature,* p. 120, note 12.

NOTES TO CHAPTER V

[1] R. M. Wenley, *Kant and his Philosophical Revolution,* p. 273.

[2] See the statements of Ludwig Ernst Borowski, *Darstellung des Lebens und Charakters Immanuel Kants,* pp. 98—101, on Kant's failure to grasp the depths of Christianity; cf. also Reinhold Bernhard Jachmann, *Immanuel Kant geschildert in Briefen an einen Freund* in the same volume as the work of Borowski (see Ch. IV, note 116 above), pp. 176—181.

[3] *Critique of Pure Reason,* pp. 338—360.

[4] See Ch. II, notes 16—24, above.

[5] The phrase is Reinhold Niebuhr's.

[6] See the brilliant analysis of Idealism in H. A. Korff, *Geist der Goethezeit,* I, *Sturm und Drang* (Leipzig, 1923), pp. 32—59.

[7] Wilhelm Luetgert, *Die Religion des deutschen Idealismus und ihr Ende* (4 vols., 2nd ed.; Gütersloh, 1923—1930).

[8] Richard Kroner, *Von Kant bis Hegel* (2 vols.; Tübingen, 1921—1924).

[9] On the relative merits of the two terms, cf. Wilhelm Windelband, *Einleitung in die Philosophie* (Tübingen, 1914), pp. 126—129.

[10] Korff, *op. cit.,* pp. 45—59, lists several stages through which its ideology passed, each one actually a complex of several elements.

[11] On some of the difficulties involved in placing Idealism into its historical setting and in isolating its distinctive tenets, cf. Horace L. Fries, "A Note on the Interpretation of German Idealism" in *Studies in the History of Ideas,* II (New York, 1925), pp. 255—272.

[12] Ch. IV, notes 89—94, above.

13 The most penetrating brief analysis I know of seventeenth-century mechanism is Alfred North Whitehead's chapter on "The Century of Genius," *Science and the Modern World* (New York, 1926), pp. 57—82; on the eighteenth century, see the following chapter, pp. 83—108.

14 Cf. M. P. Cushing, *Baron d'Holbach. A Study in Eighteenth-Century Radicalism in France* (New York, 1914) for an interpretation.

15 On part of this problem, see Ch. IV, notes 131—133, above.

16 Cf. Charles Sibree's "Translator's Introduction" to Hegel's *The Philosophy of History* (revised edition; New York, 1944), pp. iii—iv on the difficulty of finding an adequate English rendering for *Geist*.

17 Ch. IV, note 120, above; see also Whitehead's comment, *Science and the Modern World*, pp. 199—200: "The philosophers who developed the Kantian school of thought, or who transformed it into Hegelianism, either lacked Kant's background of scientific knowledge or lacked his potentiality of becoming a great physicist if philosophy had not absorbed his main energies."

18 Cf. the illuminating discussion of John Veitch, "Dualism and Monism, or, Relation and Reality" in *Essays in Philosophy*, Second Series (Edinburgh, 1895), pp. 1—116.

19 My discussion of this problem owes much to the presentation of Rudolf Eucken, *Main Currents of Modern Thought*, translated by Meyrick Booth (New York, 1912), pp. 215—239.

20 William James, *A Pluralistic Universe*, Hibbert Lectures 1909 (New York, 1943), p. 72.

21 For a valid form of theological dualism, see the comments of Edgar Carlson, *The Reinterpretation of Luther*, pp. 48—57.

22 Hans Flöter, *Die Begründung der Geschichtlichkeit der Geschichte in der Philosophie des deutschen Idealismus* (Halle, 1936); on *Geist*, esp. pp. 96—131.

23 Cf. the analysis of George Wehrung, "Theologie und deutscher Idealismus," *Zeitschrift für systematische Theologie*, IX, (1931—1932), pp. 181—210.

24 Charles Carroll Everett, *Fichte's Science of Knowledge. A Critical Exposition* (Chicago, 1892), is a fair and intelligible summary.

25 For Spinoza's philosophy of religion and its influence on the pantheism of post-Kantian philosophers, see notes 83—85 below.

26 See Kant's repudiation of Fichte, dated August 7, 1799, *Werke*, VIII, pp. 600—601.

27 Cf. William Smith, "Memoir of Fichte," prefaced to the English translation of *Johann Gottlieb Fichte's Popular Works* (London, 1873), pp. 37—50, on the background and argument of this work.

[28] On Kant's influence upon the *Kritik aller Offenbarung*, see Robert Adamson, *Fichte* (Philadelphia, 1881), pp. 25—35; also Kant's statement of July 3, 1792, *Werke*, VIII, p. 595.

[29] Ch. IV, notes 135—138, above.

[30] William Smith, *op. cit.*, pp. 60—63, on Fichte's doctrine of God.

[31] *The Vocation of Man* is reprinted in *Johann Gottlieb Fichte's Popular Works*, pp. 235—379.

[32] *The Vocation of Man, ibid.*, pp. 364—366.

[33] This was, of course, Spinoza's doctrine, to which Fichte had earlier been attracted.

[34] *The Vocation of Man, Popular Works*, pp. 360—361; cf. also Lecture IX of *The Doctrine of Religion, Popular Works*, pp. 520—534.

[35] Johann Eduard Erdmann, *Grundriss der Geschichte der Philosophie*, II, p. 464.

[36] The section on "Doubt," pp. 237—265; on "Knowledge," pp. 266—311, on "Faith," pp. 312—379, of *The Vocation of Man*.

[37] Ch. III, notes 123—136, above.

[38] Ch. IV, notes 134—139, above.

[39] Cf. the witty comments of Josiah Royce, *The Spirit of Modern Philosophy* (2nd ed.; Boston, 1920), pp. 183—186, on Schelling's ridiculing of Fichte's egocentric bias.

[40] Erdmann, *op. cit.*, II, pp. 501—530, has presented a careful exposition of Schelling's confusing development.

[41] There is a sensitive analysis of Schelling's relations to the Romantic school in Oskar Walzel, *German Romanticism*, translated by Alma Elise Lussky (New York, 1932), pp. 51—70.

[42] On the effects of this, cf. Elert, *Morphologie*, II, pp. 155—157.

[43] Richard Kroner has summarized Schelling's attempts at a system in his *Von Kant bis Hegel*, I, pp. 535—592.

[44] Cf. John Watson, *Schelling's Transcendental Idealism. A Critical Exposition* (Chicago, 1882), pp. 218—236, for an analysis of Schelling's God, with attention also to his affinities with Spinoza.

[45] See notes 69 ff. below.

[46] Watson, *op. cit.*, p. 90 ff., on Schelling's nature philosophy.

[47] See the work of Hans Flöter, referred to in note 22 above, on the significance of the philosophy of history for the thought of Idealism.

[48] Paul Tillich has indicated Schelling's relationship to modern existentialism in his essay "Existential Philosophy," *Journal of the History of Ideas,* V, (1944), p. 68.

[49] See the exceedingly sympathetic account of Edward Caird, *Hegel* (Philadelphia, 1883).

[50] Georg Wilhelm Friedrich Hegel, *Early Theological Writings,* translated by T. M. Knox (Chicago, 1948).

[51] "Introduction" to Hegel's *Early Theological Writings,* p. 53.

[52] Wilhelm Dilthey, "Die Jugendgeschichte Hegels," *Gesammelte Schriften,* IV (Leipzig and Berlin, 1925).

[53] *Early Theological Writings,* pp. 67—181.

[54] See notes 87—91 below.

[55] Thus in Hegel's own profession, *Positivity,* p. 68: "that the aim and essence of all true religion, our religion included, is human morality, and that all the more detailed doctrines of Christianity, all means of propagating them, and all its obligations . . . have their worth and their sanctity appraised according to their close or distant connection with that aim."

[56] So, for example, the entire section on "The Form Morality Must Acquire in a Church," *ibid.,* pp. 135—142.

[57] *The Spirit of Christianity and Its Fate* (1798—1799), *Early Theological Writings,* pp. 182—301.

[58] *Spirit of Christianity,* pp. 210—224.

[59] Cf. Ch. IV, notes 134—139; Ch. V, notes 35—39, above.

[60] Karl Barth, *Die protestantische Theologie,* pp. 343—378.

[61] On Hegel's relation to Kant and Fichte, cf. Caird, *op. cit.,* pp. 112—133.

[62] On Hegel and Schelling, *ibid.,* pp. 45—64.

[63] *Ibid.,* pp. 57—64.

[64] Royce, *op. cit.,* pp. 214—216, has discussed Hegel's God.

[65] *Ibid.,* pp. 201—202.

[66] Hegel thus tried to steer clear of an immanentism that borders on pantheism, and of a doctrine of transcendence that is dangerously close to Deism.

[67] Georg Wilhelm Friedrich Hegel, *The Philosophy of History,* translated by J. Sibree (revised edition; New York, 1944), p. 318 ff.; see, *e. g.,* p. 319: "God is thus recognized as Spirit, only when known as the Triune."

[68] On Hegel's philosophy of history, see the penetrating comments of Paul Barth, *Die Geschichtsphilosophie Hegels und der Hegelianer* (Leipzig, 1925).

[69] *The Philosophy of History,* p. 331, on John's Gospel.

[70] Hegel's view of history is subjected to careful examination by John Veitch in his essay "History and the History of Philosophy," *Essays in Philosophy, Second Series,* pp. 136—173, esp. pp. 154—173, on "What remains of the Hegelian view?"

[71] With the vividness that marks his entire presentation, Veit Valentin has described the sweep of Hegel's philosophy of history and its political significance, *The German People,* pp. 370—371.

[72] Otto George von Simson uses this very phrase of Goethe to help explain Christian liturgy: "Das abendländische Vermächtnis der Liturgie" in Arnold Bergsträsser (ed.), *Deutsche Beiträge zur geistigen Ueberlieferung,* p. 5.

[73] Cf. Brunner's chapters on "Myth, History, and Revelation" in *Revelation and Reason,* pp. 396—412, and on "The 'Mythology' of Christianity" in *The Mediator,* pp. 377—396, for a stimulating exposition of this thesis, especially on the difference between Christianity and Idealism on this point.

[74] On Schleiermacher's life and thought, see the outstanding exposition of Wilhelm Dilthey, *Leben Schleiermachers,* edited by H. Mulert (Berlin, 1922).

[75] For Orthodoxy, see Ch. III, note 66 ff. above; for Rationalism, Ch. IV, notes 44—46, and *passim.*

[76] Emil Schürer, *Schleiermachers Religionsbegriff und die philosophischen Voraussetzungen desselben* (Leipzig, 1868), p. 21 ff.

[77] Emil Brunner, *Die Mystik und das Wort* (Tübingen, 1924), is as sharp a criticism of Schleiermacher as has appeared in recent years; in it Schleiermacher emerges as the archheretic of modern Protestantism.

[78] Schleiermacher's debt to the romantic tradition is assessed by Robert M. Wernaer, *Romanticism and the Romantic School in Germany* (New York, 1910), pp. 143—150; though in some ways outdated, Wernaer's treatment is useful for the obvious sympathy with which he seeks to understand German Romanticism.

[79] In addition to the work of Oskar Walzel, *German Romanticism,* referred to in note 42 above, and Wernaer's study, referred to in note 78, see Paul Martin Bretscher, *The History and Cultural Significance of the Taschenbuch "Urania"* (Chicago, 1936), pp. 71—82.

[80] A leading modern classicist, Werner Jaeger, has discussed the work of Schleiermacher on Plato in his *Paideia: the Ideals of Greek Culture,* translated by Gilbert Highet, II, *In Search of the Divine Centre* (New York, 1943), p. 78; also p. 383, note 8.

[81] On philosophy and theology in Schleiermacher, cf. the remarks of Karl Dunkmann, *Die theologische Prinzipienlehre Schleiermachers* (Gütersloh, 1916), pp. 19—25.

82 For a detailed analysis of Schleiermacher's doctrine of God, see Eugen Franzenburg. *Absolutheit, Geistigkeit und Persönlichkeit bei Schleiermacher* (Berlin, 1902); also helpful for an interpretation of the *Reden über die Religion* — I have used the edition of Berlin, 1859 — is Emil Fuchs, *Schleiermachers Religionsbegriff und religiöse Stellung zur Zeit der ersten Ausgabe der Reden* (Giessen, 1901), pp. 74—81.

83 Cf. Richard McKeon, *The Philosophy of Spinoza. The Unity of his Thought* (New York, 1928), pp. 313—317, for a critical but sympathetic evaluation; see also Albert Lawkowitz, "Die religionsphilosophische Bedeutung des Spinozismus," *Kant-Studien,* XXXII (1927), pp. 151—160.

84 McKeon has interpreted the term against its medieval background, *ibid.,* p. 69, note 28.

85 The interaction of theology and philosophy in Schleiermacher is treated in most of the works mentioned in previous notes; cf., in addition, Hermann Mulert, *Schleiermacher-Studien,* I, *Schleiermachers geschichtsphilosophische Ansichten in ihrer Bedeutung für seine Theologie* (Giessen, 1907), pp. 19—46.

86 Cf. J. L. Neve, *A History of Christian Thought,* II (Philadelphia, 1946), pp. 122—126 for a brief account of this influence.

87 David Friedrich Strauss, *The Life of Jesus Critically Examined,* translated from the fourth German edition by George Eliot (5th ed.; London, 1906), esp. the introductory discussion of mythus, pp. 1—92, on criteria for discerning the historical in the mythological. See also Albert Schweitzer, *The Quest of the Historical Jesus,* pp. 68—120.

88 See the remarks of Eduard Füter, *Geschichte der neueren Historiographie* (3rd ed.; München and Berlin, 1936), pp. 431—442; on Baur, pp. 439—441.

89 On Martensen, cf. Reidar Thomte, *Kierkegaard's Philosophy of Religion* (Princeton, 1948), p. 6 ff.

90 Samuel Štefan Osuský, *Filozofia Štúrovcov* (3 vols.; Myjava, 1926—1932), I, pp. 23—28; II, pp. 127—133.

91 See Elert's profound discussion of German Idealism under the title "Deutschtum als säkularisiertes Luthertum," *Morphologie des Luthertums,* II, pp. 145—158. The precise statement on p. 152 is worth quoting in full: "Wieder kommen die Gestalter der neuen Epoche des deutschen Denkens Fichte, Schelling, Hegel vom Studium unserer Theologie her. Und sie gingen nicht hindurch, um sich in dumm-dreister Aufgeklärtheit nachher effektvoll vor ihr abheben zu wollen. Sie bohrten sich vielmehr ein in die Urfragen der Theologie Luthers, ohne freilich ganz zu ermessen, dasz die beherrschende übergreifende Dynamik in dieser ihren Ursprung hatte. Aber tatsächlich rangen sie wie Abraham und Jakob in Luthers Genesisvorlesung mit dem Deus absconditus."

⁹² The most concise summary of Kiergegaard's thought known to me is the essay by Melville Chaning-Pearce in Donald Attwater (ed.), *Modern Christian Revolutionaries* (New York, 1947), pp. 3—85. Most of his works are now available in English, thanks to the combined efforts of the Oxford and Princeton University Presses. Unusually helpful is Robert Bretall's *A Kierkegaard Anthology* (Princeton, 1946).

⁹³ See note 90 above.

⁹⁴ Cf. the biting irony in his *Concluding Unscientific Postscript to the "Philosophical Fragments,"* translated by David F. Swenson and Walter Lowrie (Princeton, 1941), pp. 317—318.

⁹⁵ Evidence of this debt is Kierkegaard's concern with the difference of time and eternity, a problem to which Hegelianism had given much attention. See the rich material offered in the detailed account by Karl Löwith, *Von Hegel bis Nietzsche* (Zürich, 1941).

⁹⁶ Chaning-Pearce, *op. cit.,* pp. 32—33.

⁹⁷ This writing, referred to in note 94 above, is the chief document of Kierkegaard's "anti-intellectualism." Philosophically, it is perhaps the most important of his works.

⁹⁸ *Concluding Unscientific Postscript,* p. 182; see also *For Self-Examination* (Oxford, 1941), p. 116.

⁹⁹ *Concluding Unscientific Postscript,* p. 118; on "being alone with God's Word," cf. *For Self-Examination,* p. 55.

¹⁰⁰ Ch. I, notes 68—104, above.

¹⁰¹ The hymnody and preaching of Lutheranism (Ch. IV, note 21) maintained the existential approach that was sometimes lost in the Church's theology.

¹⁰² Above all, in *Fear and Trembling,* translated by Walter Lowrie (Princeton, 1941).

¹⁰³ Cf. Thomte, *op. cit.,* pp. 55—62.

¹⁰⁴ *Fear and Trembling,* p. 79.

¹⁰⁵ Emil Brunner, *Die Mystik und das Wort,* seeks to contrast the subjectivity of Schleiermacher and that of the theology which the author defends against Schleiermacher; the contrast is by no means as clear as he would wish to make it.

¹⁰⁶ In addition to the points mentioned in the text, Schleiermacher and Kierkegaard share a subjective interpretation of Christianity; see note 118 below.

¹⁰⁷ *Either/Or; a Fragment of Life,* translated by David F. Swenson and Lillian Marwin Swenson (2 vols.; Princeton, 1944).

108 Cf., for example, his wistful words on "Poesy," *Concluding Unscientific Postscript,* p. 409.

109 Rudolf Otto, *The Idea of the Holy,* pp. 8—12.

110 See Thomte, *op. cit.,* pp. 16—37, on "the aesthetic stage," with liberal quotations.

111 Cf. Bernard Eugene Meland, *Seeds of Redemption* (New York, 1947), pp. 98—114, for a presentation of this viewpoint; on the Cross, pp. 109—111.

112 "The one nineteenth-century thinker of first magnitude who refused to be stampeded by the spirit of the time and saw clearly the chasm separating the sinner from God was Kierkegaard": T. A. Kantonen, *Resurgence of the Gospel,* p. 63.

113 Cf. Chaning-Pearce, *op. cit.,* p. 6.

114 *Ibid.,* pp. 36—38.

115 See the chapter on "A Creative God at Work" in Meland, *op. cit.,* pp. 49—70.

116 But when Werner Brock said almost fifteen years ago, *An Introduction to Contemporary German Philosophy* (Cambridge, 1935), p. 73, that Kierkegaard's influence "passed its zenith some time ago," he underestimated the very potentialities which he had been among the first in the English-speaking world to recognize.

117 Perhaps the outstanding example of this is Emil Brunner, whose vast theological output has been shaped more by Luther and Kierkegaard than by any other non-Biblical writers, but who has been unable to formulate any doctrine of the Church approaching that of Luther in depth and grasp of New Testament teaching.

INDEX

ALTHAUS, P., 141, n. 40

AQUINAS, TH., 3—4; 11; 124, n. 41; 128, n. 105; 139, n. 26; 146, n. 12; see also s. v. SCHOLASTICISM

ARISTOTLE, Luther's attitude toward, 4; 8; 10—12; 124, n. 40—43; Melanchthon's recovery of, 28; 31; 131, n. 26, n. 41; Melanchthon's use of, 32—35; 37—38; 133, n. 78—79; 134, passim; A. in German education, 50—51; Orthodoxy's use of Aristotelian causality, 64—65; 132, n. 51; 144, n. 93; 145, n. 94 to 97; influence on Orthodox doctrine of God, 70; 147, n. 130—135; influence on Orthodox Christology, 71—72; 148, n. 142—146; see also s. v. PLATO

ARNOLD, G., 80; 151, n. 24—25

AULEN, G., 17; 20; 126, n. 80; 128, n. 101; 135, n. 105; 140, n. 38; 146, n. 123, n. 126

BAIER, J., 63; 142, n. 59; 144, n. 83; 145, n. 94; 146, n. 118; 147, n. 141; 150, n. 8

BARTH, K., 2; 15; 21; 41; 126, n. 66; 128, n. 106; 135, n. 102; 155, n. 82; 156, n. 101; 157, n. 113, n. 122; 162, n. 60

BENGEL, J., 82; 141, n. 48; 152, n. 41

BENTE, F., 129, n. 4; 130, n. 12; 134, n. 87; 135, n. 98; 136, n. 117

BOEHME, J., 80; 106; 151, n. 23

BOEHMER, H., 122, n. 14; 127, n. 98; 128, n. 109; 138, n. 4

BORNKAMM, H., 122, n. 16; 151, n. 23

BRETSCHER, P., 163, n. 79

BROCK, W., 166, n. 116

BRUNNER, E., 1; 17—19; 22; 41; 82; 116; 121, n. 1; 125, n. 55; 126, n. 66, n. 79; 127, n. 93; 128, n. 116; 135, n. 100; 147, n. 139—140; 153, n. 45; 163, n. 73, n. 77; 165, n. 105; 166, n. 117

CAEMMERER, R., 35; 130, n. 16, n. 23; 133, n. 66—67; 136, n. 111

CALIXTUS, G., 26; 130, n. 13; 151, n. 17

CALOV, AB., 56; 57—58; 85; 140, n. 35; 141, passim; 144, n. 79; 148, n. 154

CALVIN, J., and CALVINISM, 22; 45; 55—57; 136, n. 124; 141, n.. 39, n. 41; 148, n. 147; see also s. v. GROTIUS

CARLSON, E., 126, n. 77; 127, n. 88; 129, n. 119; 130, n. 15; 134, n. 86; 146, n. 123; 160, n. 21